A True Man For Others

A True Man For Others

The Coach Jim Cotter Story

By Jim Cotter
With Paul Kenney

Published by Jetty House
An imprint of Peter E. Randall Publisher
Portsmouth, NH

Published by Jetty House
An imprint of Peter E. Randall Publisher
Box 4726, Portsmouth, NH 03802-4726
www.perpublisher.com

(ISBN13) 978-0-9817898-3-5
(ISBN10)0-9817898-3-8

Library of Congress Control Number: 2009935892

Website:
http://www.coachjimcotter.com

Cover photo by Hornick/Rivlin Studio

Photo credits for some of the photo section:
John Gillooly
Alice Poltorick
Grace Cotter Regan

Book design and composition by Ed Stevens Design
www.edstevensdesign.com

CONTENTS

PROLOGUE

The following is an excerpt from the March 8, 2007 introduction by Grace Cotter Regan on the occasion of her dad's acceptance of Boston College High School's Saint Ignatius Award.

One of my father's role models was Lou Gehrig, which in light of his recent diagnosis, is quite ironic.

Gehrig was one of the most naturally talented baseball players in history, but he wasn't always remembered or recognized for his talent. He was just as often remembered for his humility, and the way he always conducted himself, namely, as a gentleman.

One of Gehrig's famous quotes is, "Let's face it. I'm not a headline guy. I always knew that as long as I was following the Babe to the plate, I could have gone up there and stood on my head. The Babe is one fellow, and I am another, and I could never be exactly like him. I don't try. I just go on going in my own right."

Well, that description is a perfect fit for my Dad. Jim Cotter is not a "headline guy" and he has been in the shadow of a lot of headline guys. Like Lou Gehrig, he always knew who he was, what he valued, and did what had to be done. He always did things for one reason, simply because it was the right thing to do. It wasn't for kudos, fanfare, or applause and it was usually for the betterment of someone else. And just like Gehrig, he just kept on going, and doing things the right way."

—Grace Cotter Regan

INTRODUCTION

By Paul Kenney

Jim Cotter exudes a presence that is as sharp, and multifaceted, as the predominantly Irish-Catholic neighborhoods of his home town of Dorchester. In his day, Savin Hill was the bluest of blue-collar neighborhoods, a tightly packed community of machinists, stevedores, and laborers who patronized the local tavern during the week and the parish church on Sunday. It was here that Jim Cotter earned his Ph.D. in life experience. His character was molded by a strong-willed longshoreman father, an influential parish priest, and the playing fields and street corners of his youth. Even though he may have physically left nearly 50 years ago, in Jim Cotter the heart of Savin Hill still beats strongly. His experiences there shaped him as a man and help explain, what some feel, is a complex personality.

For some who know him, the words salty, outspoken, and tough best describe this forceful bear of a man. Those who have been coached or counseled by him might be inclined to use kind, caring, and firm.

The one moniker that needs no clarification, and one that he has worn proudly for 41 of his 72 years, is "Coach."

During his 44-year tenure at Boston College High School as a history teacher, guidance counselor, and coach of baseball, basketball, and, most notably, football, Cotter has evolved into the secular face of this Jesuit academic giant that sits at the edge of Dorchester Bay on the South Boston/Dorchester line.

Cotter, a class of 1955 graduate, returned to his alma mater on a professional basis in 1960, the year that John Fitzgerald Kennedy captured the White House. In those idealistic days, he was a freshly scrubbed 23-year-old graduate of Boston College who sported a whiffle haircut, walked with a cocksure John Wayne strut, and had a tenuous grasp of American history, the course he'd been hired to teach. Cotter's rise to prominence came when he took over the football program in 1964. He would hold the school's title of Coach longer than most dictators hold office.

Cotter's Massachusetts High School Hall of Fame football coaching career (236-149-17), which included two state championships, began the same year that the Beatles performed on the *Ed Sullivan Show,* that Cassius Clay defeated Sonny Liston for the World Heavyweight Title, and that a 35-year-old civil rights leader, by the name of Martin Luther King, was awarded the Nobel Peace Prize.

Some four decades, and nine presidents, later, two of the Beatles along with Ed Sullivan and Martin Luther King are no longer with us, Cassius Clay long ago changed his name to Muhammad Ali, and the freshly scrubbed Cotter of 1960 is now a seasoned member of Club AARP. After 41 years of fighting football wars, Jim Cotter finds himself in the toughest battle of his life. He is battling ALS, Amyotrophic Lateral Sclerosis, otherwise known as Lou Gherig's disease.

The root of this memoir started from a simple phone call. Word had circulated that Coach had been diagnosed with ALS. I was one of the countless legions who reached out to express care and concern. In the course of our conversation, Jim mentioned that he should write a book. I was intrigued by the idea.

A few months later, in February 2007, I called again. I reminded the coach of our conversation and told him I was just the man for the project. He accepted unconditionally. For the next nine months, Coach Cotter and I met every Friday, talking in the living room of his comfortable home in Quincy, Massachusetts.

During the course of those conversations, I watched Coach slowly regress from using a cane, then a walker, to finally being confined to a battery-powered wheelchair. In all that time, I never heard a word of regret or self-pity.

I also received an education. Those conversations richly detailed an era long past, and painted the portrait of a vibrant, colorful, and well-lived life. It was during those Friday chats that I also realized what a significant role this man, a singular son of Savin Hill, has played in the lives of so many. As proud as he is of being a coach, Jim Cotter is much more than that. He is a father, husband, teacher, athlete, counselor, athletic director, and, most important, loyal friend, who keeps a keen eye trained for the underdog.

In his four decades of service to BC High, Cotter grew to become the iconic, secular face of that Jesuit institution. In fact, the only titles he hasn't held are school president and priest. But beneath his vigorous and steely exterior, beats a heart that is fueled by the simple desire to help others. It is what truly defines Jim Cotter, the man.

As you will read in this memoir, Cotter directed many of "his kids" into better colleges, and, ultimately, onto a clearer path toward success. One of his students, for example, was literally living in his car. Through Jim's guidance, the boy went onto become president of his college class.

That's the reason for this book: so Jim Cotter can tell his stories. And through those stories, he is telling the story of every young boy who passed his way and was touched by the example of this man. The days of jackets and ties, brush-cut hair, and measured sideburns on Morrissey Boulevard may be over, but the spirit of the man from Savin Hill still burns bright. Jim Cotter truly is: A Man for Others.

CHAPTER ONE

COTTER'S WAY

I'm Jim Cotter, and I'm dying of ALS.

More commonly known as Lou Gehrig's disease, it is a progressive, chronic disease of the nerves that originate from the spinal cord. Those nerves are responsible for supplying electrical stimulation to the muscles, which are necessary for the movement of your body parts.

I was diagnosed in October 2006. When you hear those words directed at you it is sort of a shock, but it wasn't anything scary. I just reacted to it like I take all things, good or bad: in a matter-of-fact manner. I've heard some people refer to my way of handling things as the "Cotter Way." I never felt sorry for myself. What am I going to do, sit around and brood about my problem?

I began feeling a weakness in my legs in the fall of 2004, my last official year of coaching. It was just a weakness; I was still able to go out for a walk along the Wollaston Beach boulevard, but my legs were just not as strong. After I retired, I continued to go to the Y in Quincy for a daily workout. It wasn't until late 2005 that I experienced my first physical problems.

I fell three times walking into the Y, all within a period of a couple of months. After the third fall, I sought medical advice. Initially, they thought it might be something connected to my spine, but after that was ruled out, they focused on the neuro-logical aspects, and that's when I was diagnosed with ALS, in Oc-tober 2006. The disease didn't affect my retirement plans. Agnes and I had no desire to winter in Florida, but we were determined to maintain our active lifestyle.

It's never been easy for me to talk about myself. I guess that's from the way I was brought up in my neighborhood of Savin Hill. But I want people to know what made me who I am. I want them to know what's been important to me, and what I'm proudest of. And maybe the best way to do that is to begin at the end: my last game as Head Football Coach of Boston College High School.

The date of my last game was November 24, 2004; it was against our long-time rival, Catholic Memorial, whom we have played every Thanksgiving since 1962. We played at Alumni Sta-dium on the campus of my alma mater, Boston College. For many years, the schools have played on Thanksgiving eve, so everyone could be at home with their families on the holiday itself, which I think is a great idea.

When the day arrived, I knew I was going to miss coaching. I knew it was right to leave because of my health, but I still didn't want to give it up. The last four years—during which I had been able to "retire" from my responsibilities as a guidance counselor so I could concentrate on football—had been a pure joy. Despite three losing seasons, we still had great kids, and I relished going to work every day.

Anyway, back to that night. We did our pre-game warm-ups and went back into the locker room. Then we brought the sen-iors back out early because in their final high school game, we al-ways introduce the seniors of both teams. Well, when I came back out, I looked down to the left end zone and under the goal posts were 35 of my former captains from the last 40 years. I had no idea. I thought, what the hell is this!

That group included my two original captains from 1964, Paul Saba and Steve Ranere, who both went to Harvard, and played in the famous 1968 Harvard/Yale game, in which one of the newspapers carried the screaming headline: "Harvard Beats Yale 29-29." So I went over to the end zone, shook hands, and had a brief conversation with everybody. Then the captains formed two lines at midfield and asked me to pass through. My entire family joined us. It was really nice. That's when it hits you—you're not going to be doing this anymore.

That night, my offensive coordinator Mark Stonkus insisted I call all the plays. I initially balked, but he was adamant, saying, "That is what you used to do," and after thinking about it, I did.

Even though we lost that game 7-6, when the gun sounded, I felt like the luckiest guy in the world. I thought about all these friends, all these players, who, even though I may not have seen them for years, I know cared, cared for me and cared for the program. Having my whole family there, I thought about how lucky I was to have three great kids and a lovely wife. That's what I was thinking.

After the game, I went to the bus along with the rest of the coaches to collect the uniforms, and we shook hands with every kid. I remember the kids were very subdued, so I made it clear that it was just another game as far as I was concerned. I said, "Look, tomorrow the sun is going to come up, and I'm going to get up and get a coffee and a doughnut, and you're going to get up and go on with your life, so don't worry about me. I'm fine."

One of my players came up and apologized for the loss and asked me how I was going to be with this. I told him, "I'm fine, I'm going out to have a couple of beers at the Eire Pub," and the kid laughed and said he wouldn't expect anything less. So I took my entire family and we went down to the Eire. There were about 20 of us sitting in the far corner of the room, and that was the final chapter to my 41-year coaching career at BC High. I can't complain about a thing; I had a great ride.

CHAPTER TWO

LIKE FATHER, LIKE SON

One of the guys from my Savin Hill neighborhood, Danny Ryan, has a saying that is particularly appropriate to understanding my relationship with my dad: "If it's in the cat, it's in the kitten."

In my case, the cat was my father, George Lesley Cotter, who, unless you wanted a left hand to the chops, only answered to Les.

Fathers were all the same back in the late '40s and '50s. They never participated in anything involving the household. In today's world, these fathers might be looked upon in a negative way, but in those days, fathers did one of two things: They either came home for dinner or stopped into the barroom after work, staggered home, and fell asleep.

Les fell into the dinner category. He worked a full day on the waterfront, came home to our third-floor apartment, ate dinner, watched some television, and didn't spend a lot of time interacting with us kids. Here's an example: My father was third-string catcher for the Boston Braves, but Dad could make more money in the New England League playing regularly for the Pawtucket club than he could in the major leagues. Unfortunately, the Pawtucket club folded because of the Depression, and that put an end to his baseball career. I played catch every day, but never once with my father. I might have been a better baseball player than a football player, and he could have taught me everything there is to know about catching, but that was just the way he was.

Whatever my father gave my mother for money during the week, which sometimes wasn't very much, she had to make do. I made a vow that I would never be like that. In fact, one of the first things my two brothers and I did when we went into the workforce was to buy our own homes. Like most fathers in the neighborhood, my dad never had a bank account and never considered owning a house. He didn't want, or need, that responsibility.

Hating the Pressure, Turning to Drink

Dad owned a car, but it was always a crappy one, and, like I said, he never owned a house. Dad was a stevedore on the docks, which means that when a ship came in, it was his job to organize the gangs to unload it. If he'd had his way, I don't think he would have ever become a stevedore. He would have remained a gang boss, where you're in control of your gang and that's it; there's no responsibility to speak of. But when you're a stevedore, if a ship doesn't get out in 20 hours, you lose money. Somebody is going to be on your butt, and that pressure started to affect him.

Dad would start drinking every time a ship came in, but between ships, he wouldn't drink. It was just the responsibility of running the ship and running the men. He needed a little fortification in him. Not that he was afraid of anything; he just hated the responsibility. Many times Dad would be sober when the ship came in, and drunk when it left. He'd go down to the captain's office, and the captain of the ship always loved the stevedore. The captains knew that without the cooperation of the stevedore, they would never get offloaded on schedule, and that was their priority, to get offloaded and back to sea. So the captains took good care of the stevedores.

My father loved to drink Scotch. That was his drink. I never saw him drink a beer. And, for the most part, he could hold it. One time at a Knights of Columbus party, I saw him drink an entire quart of Scotch in one sitting, and he was ultimately more sober than anyone at the place. I think he was about 50 years old at the time. As he got older, it began to catch up with him, but, like I said, he wasn't a responsible guy.

The Boxer

My father was five-foot-eleven, 220 pounds, and he could hit like a mule. He could fight like a professional. I guess that's how I ended up rather proficient with my hands. My mother, just before she passed away, gave me a shirt box full of pictures. I pulled out one that caught my eye. It was a photo of my father and two other guys, and all of them were wearing black topcoats and big soft homburg hats. I had no idea who the other two guys were. Well, one night shortly before he died, my father, who at the time was stricken with Alzheimer's, was over the house with my brother Francis. I pulled that picture out and asked him to identify the other two guys. He had a moment of clarity that made it seem like yesterday. He pointed to one of the guys and said, "That's Mugsy." I forget who he said the other one was. He told me that they were going to fight over in East Boston. He told me that he was fighting heavyweight, and that Mugsy was fighting middleweight, and that the other guy was their corner man. In those days they had fight clubs all over the place, little gyms, school halls, and you could pick up a few bucks, maybe 10 if you won the fight, which back then was pretty good money. And boxing was one of the nation's biggest sports.

My father was offered a scholarship to play football at St. John's Prep, which at the time was a boarding school. He was an 18-year-old kid playing in the Boston Park League, and whoever was the coach at Fordham back then heard about Les and offered him a scholarship if he completed one year at St. John's. He was a great fullback—220 pounds and he ran with a high knee action. He'd run through the line, and guys would bounce off him, but the last thing he wanted to do was go to school, so he never followed through.

My father grew up in a three-decker on the corner of Mount Vernon Street and Boston Street in Dorchester, in the Edward

Everett Square section of the city. Grampa Cotter, my grandfather, was a veterinarian and the father of 11 children. He also had a kennel in the cellar, in which he raised and sold Boston Terriers. One day my uncle Eddie, who was my father's youngest brother, comes running into the house. Now, at the time, my grandfather was bedridden with arthritis. Anyway, Eddie runs in and says that Uncle Jim, for whom I'm named, was just beat up by a police officer, a guy who had a reputation of being a real nasty horse's-behind. So my grandfather called Les over to his side. He told Les to go down to the corner, wait for the cop, and then take care of the situation. Grandpa Cotter told Les that if he did that, he would probably have to get out of town for a while.

Les follows his instructions, and beats the hell out of the cop, and puts the guy in the hospital. And now, he's got to get out of town. My grandfather studied veterinary medicine down in Washington, D.C., so he sent Les down to a former classmate's house in D.C., where he stayed for two years.

I believe it was Congressman John McCormack who got it to blow over. He was a good friend of my grandfather, and his office was also in his home in Edward Everett Square, at the corner of Massachusetts Avenue and Columbia Road, which was right around the corner from my grandfather's house. Les's exile actually worked out all right because for the two years that he was down in the Baltimore-D.C. area, he started working on the docks and learned the time-honored trade of a being a longshoreman, which would play a significant role in my early working years and in the development of my work ethic.

Champion of the Underdog

Even though my dad was one tough son-of-a-gun, he was also a very humble man, as well as a champion of the underdog. If he could help out anyone he deemed less fortunate, he would do it, sometimes at my expense. That's probably where I developed my instinct for helping get kids into college.

One of the ways Dad displayed that kindness was his regular

visits to the "joint" to see a pair of local neighbors who were "away." Tommy Ballou was a bad guy from Charlestown who was doing time in Walpole, but what he had done didn't matter, because he was a pal of my father's, and Les went to visit him in the can all the time. When Tommy was released from Walpole, my dad picked him up at the gate and got him a job on a fishing boat, which went out to sea for six weeks. Tommy always kept the pay stub in his wallet, and every time he'd see me he'd break out the stub, waving it over his head, and then he'd yell, "Jimmy, six weeks on the seas and $27.58." Then he'd laugh, shake his head, and add, "Ridiculous, but your father got me back into the world with good people again, and I'll always be grateful."

Another guy my dad visited in jail was one of my pals from the corner, who was my age and was shot in a robbery attempt. I don't want to use his name, but he tried to hold up Matty Landy's package store in Southie. Unfortunately for him, an off-duty cop was in the back having a couple of beers before he went home. The cop hears the commotion, comes out from the back, and tells my pal to drop the gun. He turns around toward the cop, and that's when the cop shot him in the stomach. He ended up in Walpole and my father was up there every other week to visit him. He loved the guy.

As I mentioned, sometimes Dad's acts of kindness were at my expense. One of those that still resonates occurred one night on the waterfront. Bobby Noonan was my father's first wag, or scalawag, which meant if there was an opening for a worker, he would be chosen first. But I was his kid, and I thought that should count for something. On this particular night Bobby and I faced him together. "Facing" means just like it sounds: You went down to the dock and faced the stevedore, hoping to be chosen for a job slot. I often faced my father with Bobby, and, usually, he'd have more than one job. That night, I stood with a dozen or so guys facing him, but he only had one job. "Bobby Noonan, third gang, that's it. That's all. Go home," Dad said. I went up to him and said, "What about me?" He told me, "Look, he's got 10 kids, don't worry about it, go home."

Another example involved a Red Sox game, the sport my father loved. Joe Sheehan, a neighbor, and I, were sitting on the front stairs. We were in high school at the time. My father came home one day and had tickets to an afternoon Red Sox game. He asks, "Joe, do you want to go to the game?" Of course, Joe said yes. "Hop in," Dad said, and off they went.

Dad left me sitting on the front stairs. I remember saying to my mother, "Jeez, Daddy took Joe and didn't take me." My mother said, "Look, your father could only afford two tickets and Joe never has the opportunity to go to a game." She was right. The Sheehan's were probably the poorest family in Savin Hill. Although I might not have liked it at the time, that was Les, always looking out for the less fortunate.

Working on the Docks

I don't remember exactly what year it was, but, at some point, Dad became a stevedore, which was the hiring boss. It was a pretty good deal because you were on salary. So you knew you were going to get a week's pay whether you worked or not. It wasn't a lot of money; he never made any real money unless he was working overtime.

Anyway, I remember, I was 13 the first time I went to work for him. I was in the eighth grade at St. William's School, which was the neighborhood grammar school located just below the Savin Hill Bridge. I was a big kid and a little overweight. I was five-foot-eleven, about 180 pounds. The year was 1950, and one night he came home and asked if I wanted to go to work. I said sure. Then I asked, can I go down there? I'm only 13. "Of course you can, you're my kid," he said.

I went down to the docks with him, and, on my first night, we were working on bales of wool. When you're working with wool, you work with a partner. One guy would have a two-wheeler cart and you'd back into the bale; your partner would hook it and then we'd pull the cart. We're down at Castle Island working for the Moore/McCormack Shipping Company, one of the bigger firms in the area. Like I said, I'm just 13 years old. I was working with this guy named Benny Leonard, not the world champion boxer, but a professional boxer nonetheless. Benny is telling me, "I've been away, I've been away." Well, we worked together all night and got along great, but he kept telling me he's been away, but he never told me where he'd been.

When our four-hour shift ended, I got into my father's car to go home. I said, "Dad, Mr. Leonard kept talking about being away. Where was he?"

"Oh," he said, "he was in jail."

"In jail? What did he do," I asked.

"Oh, he killed a guy. Yeah, Benny was a professional fighter, and he got in a fight with a guy in a barroom, and when he hit the guy, as he was falling, he hit his head on the corner of a stool and died. Because his hands are considered weapons, he was convicted of manslaughter," Dad said.

It must have been 11:30 at night when I got home. I went to bed, but I couldn't sleep. Instead, I just stared at the ceiling all night long thinking, I just worked with a murderer.

The docks had a rule system and their own set of special codes. Each stevedore had a certain number of set gangs. There were 22 men to a gang, and there would be a sign at three or four barrooms in Southie which read: "Les Cotter has four gangs, show up at eight o'clock on Tuesday morning." The pick-up was over at the Army base, which was on the corner of D Street and Sumner, right at the entrance. Les would stand up on top of a crate and pick guys out. The regular guys, usually three gangs' worth, had everybody set. He'd go down to the ship to see who showed up, come back, and fill in any empty slots. There might be one or two jobs available if you went down to face Les.

It was an easy way to do it. Almost everybody in his first two gangs showed up all the time; those were the longshoremen's cardholders. The first gang was known as the family gang, the second gang simply the second gang, but it was interesting the way they did things in those days. We were scalawags, or nonunion. There were no scalawags in any of the regular gangs. If Les went to the ship, and there were three men missing, he'd go back to the yard and he'd have to pick up three card men. But if there were no card men there, or they just turned their backs on Les, which meant there were no card men "facing" Les, he'd be able to hire scalawags. Then, if guys didn't come back from lunch at one o'clock, the timekeeper could pick scalawags at the ship. There would usually be 10 or 12 guys standing at the ship hoping for an opening.

A Prize-winning Goat Visits Savin Hill

My father and his friends were true characters, and they were willing to do almost anything on a dare. I was 11 or 12 years old and my brother Donnie 5 or 6, when Les went down to the Marshfield Fair with some of the guys from the corner. When they got there, I think it was Deuce Dailey who dared Les to steal the goat. It had just won the blue ribbon prize at the Marshfield Fair; so on Deuce's dare, Les went ahead and stole the goat.

Now, once he's got it, he takes the goat out to the roadway to meet the car, but there's nobody there. I think the guys either left him or they thought he had gotten a ride. Now picture this, he has this prize goat, but no way to get home. He ties the goat to a tree in the woods and goes back out to the road and starts thumbing. A guy stops to pick him up, and my father asked, "Do you mind if I get my kid?"

"No, go get him," says the driver.

Les brings the goat out from the woods and they put him in the back seat and the guy drives him home all the way to Savin Hill. Now, it's in the middle of the night, and we're all asleep. Les brings the goat into our third-floor apartment and ties him to my brother Donnie's bed, then goes to sleep. Donnie and I had twin beds in the back room.

When Donnie woke up that morning, he started jumping on top of me and saying, "Jimmy, there's a pony tied to my bed." Then, of course, we had all these little marbles of goat crap all over the floor. We kept the goat tied in the backyard of the house and, for a week or two, let everybody in the neighborhood come in and pet it. Finally, one of the guys from the corner, Roger La-Montagne, said he had a relative who owned a farm in southern New Hampshire, and we gave the goat to him to take to them. I don't know what happened to the goat after that, but the guy who owned the prize-winning goat never got him back.

A Dangerous Job

Working on the docks was a dangerous job. You could get hurt anytime, plus there was always the chance that you could end up in a fight with someone, and those guys were as tough as a two-dollar steak.

I remember one night, when I was in college, I was working another half-night shift with Tommy Sullivan. Tommy was driving a tractor that would pull in the cargo once it was discharged from the ship. We were setting up to go to work, and he was pulling a save-all, which is a lattice-type rope that had been taken down from the side of the ship, and he was pulling it into the warehouse. He was going pretty fast, and as he was coming in, he just caught a two-wheeler that we were using to pull wool. Now, I don't see it, but I just happen to be standing with a bunch of guys, and as he's flying by someone yells, "Watch out!" By instinct, I jump as it catches my leg, and it tips me over and cuts my leg a little bit. Now, not only has Tommy hit Les's kid—the stevedore's son—but Tommy's also one of my Dad's best friends. Tommy thinks he's ruined my college football career. He thinks I'm an All-American, which I'm not. Anyway, he gets off the tractor and is saying, "Oh, Jesus, Jimmy, I'm so sorry. Get up and walk, try it, c'mon."

Anyway they bandaged me up and I worked the rest of the night, but if that cart had caught me right on the blade, it certainly could have cut my leg badly, broken it, or maybe something worse. From that point on, every time I saw Tommy, he'd always say, "Jim, how's the leg? Are you going to be okay?"

CHAPTER THREE

GROWING UP ON THE DOCKS

When I first was introduced to the docks, my father warned me that, to most longshoremen, "The Boss" is always considered a "moron" and to just ignore the comments. But on this one particular night, I simply reached a breaking point.

We were working another wool job, which involved pushing and pulling. I always pulled, which was harder, because I liked the work. I'm working with this gang and all night long this Italian guy is knocking Les Cotter. On the one hand, I'm listening to my dad's words, "Don't react to it." On the other hand, I'm saying screw this guy, he doesn't know what he's talking about. In my eyes, *he's* the moron, and I've got to put an end to this.

So finally I say, "Hey, shut the hell up."

"And who are you?" comes the reply.

"I'm Les's kid, and you're full of it."

"Oh, I am huh?"

"Well, your father's an A-hole!"

"Oh, he is huh? Okay, let's go."

Now, I'm thinking, this is a fistfight, and then all of a sudden this guy pulls out his hook. We all wore hooks on the side of our

13

belts. I pull out my hook, but the problem is, I don't know what the hell I'm doing with it, because I never fought with a hook before. We're dueling with the hooks, and somebody is going to get hurt bad in this fight, which is probably going to be me.

Just then Tommy Sullivan is bringing a load into the shed with his tractor, and he sees this thing going on. He leaps off the tractor and hits the guy with one punch, and all I hear is smash, down the guy goes. The guy is out like a light. Tommy says, "What's going on? Jim, why are you fighting him?" I told him he was calling my father, you know, everything in the book. He says, "Okay," unhooks the load he's hauling and tells two guys to throw the Italian on the tractor. Then he drives out of the shed. I didn't know if he was going to dump the guy in the water or what. But what he did was take him out to the entrance to Castle Island and dump him with the customs guys at the gate. He told them that if this bum wakes up, call him a cab. I never saw the guy again. Les never hired the guy again.

Booking the Dogs

There was a strike at the waterfront, it was 1961, and I was 23 years old, already teaching at BC High. Even though Les was paid a salary because of his position as stevedore, he wasn't making enough to get by.

At the same time, Eddie Connors from Connors Tavern, the neighborhood bar, decided for the first time to book the dogs. He was looking for a bookie to take bets on the greyhound races in Revere and Raynham. Back in those days, greyhound dog racing was a big sporting event, and Connors asked around for somebody to book them for him. Les had done it before, back in the '40s when he was a young kid. Joe Moakley, Sr. owned the bar that would later become Connors Tavern, and Les would fill in once in a while, when the regular bookie Vesta Byrne was either sick or took a day off. So he knew how to do it, he offered his services, and Eddie hired him.

Well, one night Gene Mack and Jerry O'Sullivan, who used to

write the police column for the Boston Globe and were friends of my father, gave me a call. They told me that they had to have a teamback (a meeting) with my father. They said we've got to talk him out of booking the dogs. They told me that, sooner or later, Joe Jordan, who later became Boston's Police Commissioner, was going to raid the place, and Jordan hated Eddie Connors.

The three of us went up to Connors and we found my father. They did all the talking. They persuaded Les that he had to give it up. They told him if he got pinched it could affect his job down at the waterfront.

It worked. My father went to Eddie and told him he had to give up the dogs. Eddie was fine with it. He replaced Les with one of my friends. My pal booked for another couple of weeks and then, just as the Globe guys predicted, the place got raided and my friend was arrested.

Sandy Richardson and the Brinks Gang

Sandy Richardson was one of the guys involved in the 1950 Brinks Building robbery. He was a good friend of my dad's. I'm not even sure how they became friendly except that it was through the waterfront. Sandy had been a sailor in World War II, and the day the FBI made the hit and arrested the Brinks' bandits, Sandy was working for my father. I'm not sure if it was at Castle Island or at the Army base, but word came down on the ship that the FBI had gotten "Big Joe" McGinnis and some of those other guys and that they were looking for Sandy Richardson.

My father took Sandy and put him in the car and took him to the corner of D Street and Summer Street in South Boston, where my uncle Red Benson managed Welby's Gas Station. My father put him in the back room and told Red to hide him there for as long as was necessary. I don't know the exact time length, but he hid him for a number of days. Of course, while all this is going on, Red is a nervous wreck figuring he's going to the federal pen for harboring a known fugitive. He figures when they get Sandy, they're going to arrest him too. Every day he'd call my father and say, "Les, you got to get him the hell out of there." So finally, Sandy himself, realizing that it was hopeless to hide out, turns himself in. Of course, he never told them where he was hiding.

The Cruelty of the Docks and a Gang of Thieves

My father was about 50 when he fell down the hold of a ship. The ship was about to sail and somebody said, "I think we left some equipment, hooks and stuff down the hold." So Les went back to check, tripped on one of the eye hooks, and fell down into the empty hold. He fell across a beam—the beam that they put down to make a false floor—and he broke all his ribs, then he proceeded to fall the remaining distance to the floor.

Fortunately, one of Les' gang bosses said, "Les hasn't come out yet." The ship was about to sail to Europe somewhere so they went in and got him, carried him out, and he ended up in the old Carney Hospital for about six weeks. He was in real bad shape, and if the ship had ever sailed he'd have been a goner.

Some of the guys working on the docks were just thieves. They were as bad as bank robbers. In fact, some of them were bank robbers. They stole everything they could get their hands on. My father never took a thing. A guy one time brought a guitar up to the house and gave it to my brother Francis, and occasionally some cans of tuna would come into the house when somebody stole an entire lot, but that was it. The docks were a crazy place. These guys lived hand to mouth, and if a ship didn't come in, they didn't get paid. It wasn't a guaranteed wage like they have now.

I'll give you some examples. One night my father made me a lander. A lander is actually two guys who take the load that comes out on a pallet and land it on the back of a tractor, unhook it, and then drive it off the dock. I always wanted to go down into the hold with the guys—we had some laughs, some fun—but we worked hard. I didn't mind working hard.

One night, this particular ship came in just after there had been a dock strike. I had just started coaching basketball at BC High, but it was school vacation, so I went down to the docks. We worked day and night. A ship would come in and we'd finish at 5 p.m., then we'd face my father and start at 7 p.m., unloading another one. The ships were backed up in the harbor because of the strike. Anyway, I go back to work the next day and Les says if I hire you, I'm going to put you as a lander in the first gang.

My father wanted me as a lander because he thought there was a customs plant on the ship, and he wanted me to watch out for the guys who might be trying to clip some merchandise. The ship we were working on was Japanese, with Japanese cargo. That meant it would have things like shoes, or Windbreakers, stuff like that.

I'm a lander in the first gang, on the second level of the Army base, and we're looking right down onto the ship and into the second hold where the box cargo is, and on this particular ship the box cargo was Windbreakers. They were those Windbreakers with the little hood and the pouch in the front; everybody had one. Anyway, Tommy Benson, Jud O'Shea, and Mugsy Whitaker are all working that day. We've got three or four loads already out and I look down and there is Benson coming up the gangplank. He's got his scally cap on, a green sweatshirt, and under the collar of the sweat shirt you can see all these different colors. He's got Windbreakers on under the sweatshirt. Now, I'm bumping into the guy we think is the plant, almost knocking him off the plank. This scene goes on almost all day. They come out; they go back down, all day long. By the end of the afternoon we go back up to Connors to grab a sandwich and a couple of beers, before we go back to work that night. Well, everybody has these Windbreakers. The guys are yelling, "Hey, give me that red in an extra-large, and toss me that blue in a medium, for my wife." We had about 400 of the things, and nobody is selling them, they're just giving them away. My father was running ragged saying, "Jeez, enough! Don't open another carton!" Of course, nobody is listening. The pilferage was incredible, and that's why the containers came into being.

Another ship, about the same time, was filled with Italian

shoes. They were pointed shoes and we used to call them spades, because they had a pointed toe. Guys would go down into the hold wearing flip-flops and come back up wearing a pair of shoes.

Another time a ship came in filled with baseball gloves. My father came aboard the ship and said to the guys down in the hold, "Look, the customs guys are all over the place. Whatever you do, don't leave the ship with a baseball glove." Of course, nobody listened. The shift ends, and the guys are coming off the ship, down the gangplank. Tommy Benson is coming down, walking behind Jud O'Shea and Bo Mullane, and they see the customs guys at the bottom of the plank. Tommy says, "Throw the gloves in the water." The unwritten rule was, that if you don't have the gloves on you, even if you are seen throwing them in the water, they can't arrest you. But they want the gloves. So they stuffed them in their bunch, which was like a pouch in the front of your jacket. As soon as they got off the ship, they get frisked, and customs finds the gloves and arrests both of them. Bo Mullane just got his notification from the Boston Police Department that he was going on the cops. But now he's under arrest by the customs agents. Les had to fix the arrest before the Boston police found out.

Anyway, we go back up to Connors that afternoon to grab the usual sandwich and a couple of beers, and my father was there. He goes over to Tommy Benson and says, "Tommy, I'm really proud of you. I told the kids the customs guys were all around the ship. Justin O'Shea and Bo Mullane, they didn't listen, and they got grabbed. You did, and I'm really proud of you."

Tommy says, "Well, Uncle Les, I got to be honest with you. I'm a lefty. There were no left-handed gloves in that shipment. If there were any lefty gloves, I would have had a couple in my bunch."

Sometimes we'd unload a meat ship, and on those days, even in the summer, the guys would come to work wearing these long overcoats and long leather jackets. Every coat would have five or six pockets on the inside. The guys would be cutting steaks and roasts and stuffing them in the pockets.

A True Lumberjack and a Fishy Caper

There was a guy on the docks who worked for my father in the family gang. My father told me that this guy built a house and cottage with stolen lumber from Castle Island. I said, "You've got to be kidding! That's an awful lot of lumber!"

One night, I'm working with him, and my father says, "Ask him if he can get you a two-foot by whatever size stick." I ask, and the guy says, "Sure. Sure. Sure." Out he goes and when he comes back he says, "I've got it," in what he called his "truck." He says, "I'll see you outside the gate, Jimmy."

Now, his truck was a car with all the seats taken out. The right side and the back seats were gone, so you could fit a 12-foot piece of lumber. He goes out at the end of the shift every night with a blanket over the lumber so you couldn't see it. Again, if it wasn't out in the open, it wasn't stealing. And as he went out the gate, he'd yell and wave, "See ya, Charlie."

Later, he built a cottage on the Cape and a home in Milton with the lumber stolen from the shipyard. Castle Island was where all the lumber came in, and this guy knew where every piece of lumber was, and whatever you needed, he could find it in a second. I don't know what my father needed it for. I think he just wanted to prove to me that the guy could do it.

My father used to work the Luckenbach Lines, and the Luckenbach line carried can goods, boxes of can goods. Some of the stuff you wouldn't bother with, but the tuna fish was like gold. Back then, a lot of people lived off it. One night, I'm working in Connors tending bar, and Tom Logan, a stevedore we used to call Uncle Tommy, came in. He was such a thief that he was eventually barred from working the waterfront. Before Connors was remodeled, it had a big picture window that looked out onto South Sydney Street, where the guys used to play half-ball.

On this particular night, I see a truck pull up and park right in front of the window. I say, "Oh, this can't be good." Connors isn't there, and I'm bartending, so I'm in charge. In comes Tom Logan. I say, "Hey, Uncle Tom, how are you?"

"Jimmy, good to see you. I'll have a ball and a beer." I'm not even sure he paid for it, the cheap so-and-so.

Then he said, "Jimmy, open the cellar door."

I said, "What for?"

He said, "I've got a load of tuna fish in the truck."

He has a whole truck full of tuna fish and he's going bar to bar to sell it to whomever he can. And he's got to get rid of it that night.

I said, "Uncle Tom, I can't open the door."

He asked, "Why not?"

I said, "If you get pinched while you're taking that stuff in the cellar, I get pinched with you as an accessory, and I can't get involved with that stuff, I'm teaching at BC High.

He said, "I'll give you a case of tuna."

"I don't need any tuna."

He said, "Your father would never forgive you."

I said, "Well, my father probably hasn't forgiven me for a lot of things, Tom, but I'm not opening that door. If Eddie [Connors] was here, he could open the door, but I'm not."

"Okay," he said, and finished his ball and beer.

He takes his truck down the street to George and Jerry's, then Tom English's, Vaughans, and any other place that would take some tuna fish. He got rid of it all, and that's the way they operated. But here I am, making 16 bucks a night, $2 an hour, working for Connors, and to risk getting arrested, not me. But I will say, he was a character.

CHAPTER FOUR

THE NEIGHBORHOOD

I was born on May 10, 1937, and grew up at 370 Savin Hill Avenue in a "six-decker" that was located in the section of Savin Hill often referred to as OTB, which means "over the bridge." Over the Bridge in Savin Hill was a working-class, blue-collar neighborhood that was dotted with a mixture of multifamily and single family homes. Unlike the streets on the other side of the bridge, which for the most part were filled with two- and three-family homes, my section of Savin Hill had a disproportionate share of single family homes, which in those days was considered a luxury. But the demographic was, for the most part, the same as the rest of the area.

The family dynamic was that mothers stayed home with the kids, and fathers took the MBTA to work. John Walsh and Mac McCarthy were the only two guys I knew who wore suits and ties to work. All the other guys who lived around me were blue collar. Red Benson worked at a gas station, Buster Connors was a linoleum layer, Frank Kelley was a fireman, Ray Gaudet worked at a factory, Joe Peecha managed a package store in Southie, and Tommy Meehan was a bookie. The Catholic grammar school, St. William's, which was our local parish, and sports, particularly the CYO, dominated everyday life. The parish church was the main artery of the neighborhood. As far as I was concerned, it was a great place to grow up. I got a Ph.D. in human nature. Growing up in the neighborhood prepared you for the world. I saw all facets of life, and I learned how to spot a phony from a mile away, which is an education that you can't put a price on.

I remember I had a fight with Billy Madden in the eighth grade at St. William's. Billy was a tough kid. We were good friends, but if we had a beef about something, we'd settle it by fighting.

We had just come back from lunch. In those days, you went home for lunch, and now we're fighting in the schoolyard after lunch. Well, the bell rings for everyone to file back into school, but we hide in the well by the stairs and when everyone is in, we continue fighting. Now, of course, there's nobody in the schoolyard, nobody to cheer me and nobody to cheer him.

Neither one of us is going to quit. One of Billy's first punches splits my lip, and I get blood all over my shirt and tie. I don't know how long we fight, but it is probably for another 15 minutes.

Our nun was Sister Patrice, and she comes down to one of the lower grades and gets one of Madden's younger brothers to find out why he isn't in class. He says, "Oh, he's out in the schoolyard, fighting with Jimmy Cotter." So she charges out into the schoolyard and drags us into Mother Superior's office. It is Sister Evangelina, and she gives us a good chewing out. But we know we're going to get more than just a chewing out. We go upstairs to the eighth grade and we're in the hall outside the classroom when Sister Patrice backs us up to the wall. She smacks me on the side of the head. I think she hits me harder than Madden did.

I say, "What are you doing, Sister?"

"You were fighting in the schoolyard," and then she turns and smacks Billy.

Now we've got to go into the classroom, and the kids are all cheering. "Hey, who won?"

"It was a draw, until Patrice got hold of us."

We were good friends before the fight, and we were good friends the rest of our lives.

Basketball in the Coal Court

Monsignor Morrisroe was our pastor when St. William's School was converted from coal heat to oil heat in 1955. Some of the guys went to Father Peter Hart, who ran the CYO, and asked if he would ask the Monsignor to give us permission to clean up the now empty coal bin and make a basketball court. We got permission, and a bunch of us spent weeks cleaning the bin. We did it by simply throwing buckets of water on the walls and sponging it down to make a court. But, needless to say, you never really got rid of all of the dust. Every day after practice, you'd blow your nose and your handkerchief would be black.

I was 18 years old at the time, and every afternoon, from three to six, five days a week, Phil Donahue, a BC student, and I coached the neighborhood kids. The size of the court was just as deep as the top of the key, so we had a basket at that wall, and it was only two-thirds the width of a regulation court. We also had a side basket, and both were regulation height. But because of the low ceiling, you couldn't really get much of an arc on a shot, particularly if you were shooting from the outside.

We had a regular group of 15 kids and I think 6 of them went on to become high school basketball captains. My brother Donnie was captain of English High for two years, Bobby Sullivan was captain of Don Bosco, Kevin Mulcahy was captain of JP [Jamaica Plain], and Joe Casey was captain of Cathedral. Teddy Ryan also played at Cathedral. And these kids were faithful. Because of the cramped quarters at St. William's, we couldn't do a lot of stuff, but we pressed like the devil. We taught them man to man press coverage, pick and roll, and taught them how to pass the ball properly. They were a terrific bunch. In the CYO League, we only lost four games in two years, and all four were to Holy Name. We lost in the Deanery Championship. Holy Name had the Costello brothers, who even though they were cadets, ages 12 and 14, they were like men.

Unfortunately, we lost our spot at the school because a pair of neighborhood kids, Arthur Sheridan and Billy Harrigan, vandalized the school. They were maybe two years older than my brother Donnie. One night, they broke into the school and took the fire extinguishers and sprayed them all over the wall. The band used to practice in one of the rooms. They didn't touch our place, which was on the lower level. But because of their ignorance, that was the end of it. It was a shame, because the court kept a lot of kids out of trouble.

A Reluctant Clarinetist

My parents wanted me to join the St. William's band when I was in the second grade. The year was either 1943 or '44, and I went down to see Sister Magdalene, who was the music director, and told her that my mother wanted me to join the band. Now, I'm a big heavy kid at the time, overweight, so I want to play something big and brassy, the bass drum or a sousaphone, something like that. But she hands me a clarinet. I tell her, "Look I don't want to play this." She tells me I have to, that it is the only way I can get into the band.

I played a clarinet for 11 years and hated every minute of it, but I enjoyed the band. I always loved music, and I loved to sing.

Shortly after I joined, maybe a year or two later, Sister Magdalene hired Dom Bianculli, who at the time was Executive Secretary of the Governor's Council. His real job was working as chief aide to the legendary Councilor Sonny McDonough. Dom took over the band. He was a great man, and I mean great with a capital G. He had such a positive influence on the kids of Savin Hill. He kept us out of trouble, kept us active, and, when we were old enough, he got us summer jobs. Heck, when Paul Dever was the governor, I was only 14 years old, but I was six-foot tall, and I guess I seemed older.

Anyway, Dom got us all jobs on the state and I remember saying to him, aren't you supposed to be 17?

He asked, "When were you born?"

I said, "1937."

"Well, tell 'em you were born in '34."

So I signed the papers 1934, and just like that, I'm now 17. I went to work stabbing papers down at Carson Beach. Some years were harder than others, but Dom still managed to get you a job.

Dom operated the band like a real drill instructor, and he taught us how to march. Before he showed up, we were just a bunch of kids who could play instruments, but when Dom came along, we became a marching band, and we were good. Two years before I stopped, they hired Dr. Herbert Silverman, from the New England Conservatory of Music, and with his hiring we finally had a music teacher. Sister Magdalene would get up there and tap her baton and maybe play the piano, stuff like that, but she didn't know music.

When Silverman came, I'd be sitting in the third row trying to hide my clarinet, playing, and making every other note the wrong note. He'd stop and say, "Mr. Cotter, play that alone." He could hear everything; he was simply outstanding. The young kids who joined the band with Silverman and Dom were so well taught that St. William's became state band champs for many years. I stayed in the band through my senior year in high school.

The Good Soul of Father Peter Hart

Father Peter Hart, who was the curate of St. William's parish during the 1950s, was one of the greatest influences on my life. I am very religious, but I never wore it on my sleeve. One time, he asked me if I knew anything about the rosary. He then explained to me the meaning of the rosary. He told me it is something you should take with you your whole life. So I became an advocate of the rosary. I try to say it everyday simply using my fingers, not the beads. Father Hart loved the Blessed Mother and the rosary. He was a great priest and a great man. It was the goodness of the man that shone through. He was the most holy man I have ever met in my life. He was probably the closest I ever came to meeting a saint in this world, or at least what you think a saint should be.

Father Hart wasn't the pastor, but he did run the CYO at St. William's, and that is why he had such a big influence on the kids in the parish. He was just a priest's priest, a man's man, and all those good things you want to say about someone. I went to Mass and communion every day all through high school, only because of Father Hart.

When I was a sophomore at BC High, he called me up one day and told me to come down to the rectory. When I arrived, he said, "I have something I want to talk to you about." He told me that he had volunteered me to serve on the CYO Speakers Bureau. Now, I'm 15 years old and he volunteered me for the CYO Speakers Bureau.

I asked, "What do they do?"

"Well, they go to communion breakfasts and sports nights and talk to the kids, stuff like that," he said.

I said, "Talk about what!?"

"We'll talk about daring to be different. You and I can write the talk. I'll give you two talks in case you go back to them the second year."

We put together a pretty good 15-minute speech, but it was the last thing I ever wanted to do. I went out and gave my first speech in my junior year, and one of my dearest friends and a high school classmate, Jack Deneen, was at the back of the parish hall at St. Elizabeth's in Milton. Deneen stood at the back of the hall for the entire speech with his middle finger up. It was things like that I feared the most. But I did it for years. It was the best experience. You couldn't buy that experience. Imagine getting up as a 16- or 17-year-old; it gave me a tremendous sense of self confidence. I stayed in the program until my junior year at Boston College.

From the Sublime to the Unsanitary

We were kids, just regular city kids, with our share of screwballs, sane guys, and everybody in between. As I mentioned, Father Hart at St. William's had a great influence on most of my gang, as well as the gang a little younger than us. He encouraged us to go to church, not just on Sunday, but during the weekday, particularly during Lent. It wouldn't be unusual for most of us, some 20 to 25 of us, to go to the 7 a.m. Mass during Lent and still make it to school. It was really impressive to see all the guys and girls walking down to church at St. William's.

I also think it brought us much closer together than we might have been. At the same time, it wasn't like we wore our religion on our sleeve. We went to church and afterwards, did our thing—went off and did all the crazy things we did. But going to Mass became part of our day, and it was really good. I think most of those guys and girls later became pretty good parents. Very few, if any, got separated or divorced. In fact, I can't think of anybody from my immediate friends who did divorce. It was a good lesson for all of us.

I was a seventh grader at St. William's, and we'd always go over and "walk the dump." The dump covered all of Columbia Point and ended up being the future home of BC High, which is located on Morrissey Boulevard across from the Boston Globe. The land was a working dump probably until 1950-'51. The bums, otherwise known as bayzos, because they drank Bay rum, used to live over there, searching through the rubble, and sometimes they would find some good stuff. When I was a kid, we always went there, and my mother used to tell me if I fell into the underground fires, I'd go straight to hell. Now, it's 1950, and the contractor is installing the girders for what was to become BC High. I remember shimmying up one of the girders and walking around the first floor, which was about eight feet up. While I was up there, this guy with a black outfit comes over, and obviously he's a priest. He gets us down off the girders, and I asked him what they were building. A school, he said. I asked him the name, and he said, "BC High."

That was the first time I ever heard of BC High, a place that would be my home for almost 50 years.

Chapter Five

THE YOUNG ATHLETE

That fall of 1950, one of my best friends, Joe Sheehan, enrolled as a freshman at BC High. In those days, students went the first two years down at Harrison Avenue, which was across the street from Boston City Hospital, and the last two years at the new school located on the boulevard. In my senior year of 1954-'55, they finally finished Cushing Hall and the entire school was officially located on the one Morrissey Boulevard campus. But it was really Joe Sheehan, who was sort of my hero, who continued to talk about how much he loved the school, plus the fact that he played football for them, that continually spiked my interest.

Sheehan, who lived two houses away, was also the kid my father took to the Red Sox game when he left me sitting on the stoop. As I mentioned, Joe was probably the poorest kid in Savin Hill. His father died when his youngest brother was one year old, and Joe was one of seven kids. I don't know how they lived. I don't think there was anything like the WIC program, and they didn't have any money. Mrs. Sheehan didn't work, and my guess is that the parish probably supported them. Joe was a great kid, a real gentleman. He started out to become a priest, but left, and got his Ph.D. in statistics at Boston College. He's worked the last 40 years as a medical statistics professor at the University of Connecticut. We're still great friends, and when I could walk, we'd play golf at the annual Savin Hill Open.

But back when we were still kids, you always tried to avoid calling Joe between 6:45 p.m. and 7 p.m., because that is when Archbishop Cushing said the rosary over the radio. If you went into Joe's house at that time, everybody was on their knees, saying the rosary.

One night I made the mistake of calling on him at that hour. When I went into the house, the entire family was on its knees. Joe's sister, Betty, who was quite a character, always knelt opposite her mother. So when I came in, I had to kneel down next to Mrs. Sheehan. Now, Mrs. Sheehan was very devout and would always have her head down, with the beads, saying the rosary. Betty would be across from me mouthing the words, "Jimmy Cotter, I love you." And before you'd know it, I'd start laughing, and everybody would be laughing, and Mrs. Sheehan would give me a little tap on the top of my head. "Stop that laughing, Jimmy Cotter." But when Joe went to BC High, that was a big influence on me and in my decision to attend the school.

I remember one night when I was an eighth-grader and we were down at the Savin Hill Yacht Club for a junior dance. It was a Friday night, and Joe Sheehan came in. Earlier that day, BC High had beaten South Boston 19-18. It was quite a victory because Southie hadn't lost a game in a couple of years. Joe came in about 10 o'clock at night and the two of us sat in the corner, and I think he told me every play from beginning to end. To this day I can still visualize it. Bill Crowley, who was a running back, breaks a tackle and Southie tackles him on the two yard line. I can remember it like it's today. The more I heard about BC High, the more I knew that was where I wanted to go.

Lessons On and Off the Court

In order to improve my clarinet playing, my mother signed me up for lessons with a nun who taught music at St. Matthew's School in Codman Square. I think that I probably went once. Every week my mother would give me the 50 cents for the lessons, and I'd head out the door, clarinet in hand. But I'd only make it as far as Carl's Drug Store, which was at the corner of Sydney Street and Savin Hill Avenue and owned by a nice guy named Carl Awed, who's still alive. I'd walk in and ask Carl if I could leave my clarinet behind the counter, then I'd buy a soda, and go down to the park and play ball with the guys. When we were finished, I'd go back to Carl's, ask if I could wash my dirty hands to hide the evidence, then head home from a hard lesson of clarinet playing. Whenever we had company at my house, my mother would make me to play the "Sheik of Araby" for everybody, but there was only one problem, I never got any better. She never said anything, but I still wonder to this day if she ever figured out that I probably never went to the lessons.

As an athlete, I knew I was good. In our gang, our crowd, I could play with the older guys and was one of the better athletes in their gang as well. I played a lot of basketball with a number of guys in the older group, who were known as the Shannons. I was 15 and they were 18, but I was six-foot-one, 190 pounds, so physically I didn't lack anything. Nobody lifted weights in those days, so strength wasn't a big difference. I could match up with those guys pretty good, and when you played with the older guys, you simply got better. They wouldn't pass you the ball unless you were open. Also, after playing with them, when you went back and played with your own gang, it was easier. I would have to say out of our group of 50 or so, as an athlete I was one of the top two kids. It would vary by sport, of course, but my best sport was football, and baseball was second.

Our basketball teams were good, but we couldn't beat the team from St. Peter's parish. One of our players was Jimmy Young, who could shoot the eyes out of the basket. He was probably our best basketball player. He had been in the seminary for a couple of years as one of those junior seminarians, and that's all they do, play basketball. When he came out, he played for Cathedral High School, which was a basketball powerhouse.

St. Peter's was a powerhouse. They had Dick Mulcahy, who

played for BC High; they also had a big fat kid by the name of McIntyre, who could shoot and score, who also played at Cathedral, and the Zmudzien brothers, who both played at Dot [Dorchester] High School. As a matter-of-fact, once a month that whole Dot High crew still gets together at Florian Hall [the Boston Firefighter's Hall] and tells lies about the old days.

My Dad, the Ego Deflator

Whenever I was feeling pretty good about myself, my father had a way of quickly shrinking my ego and bringing me right back to earth.

The best example I can give you was a football game that we, BC High, played against South Boston in 1953, at White Stadium, the now well-worn and weary schoolboy stadium located in Franklin Park in the Dorchester-Jamaica Plain section of Boston. But back in the day, it was a special place to play a football game.

In my sophomore and junior years, I played on two consecutive undefeated teams at BC High. We always played Southie, but for some reason in the '53 season, they weren't scheduled. So Joe McKenney, the director of athletics for the City of Boston, decided to create a post-season game called the "Bean Bowl," and, in the inaugural game, he pitted our undefeated BC High team against an undefeated South Boston squad. It was played on the second Saturday after Thanksgiving at White Stadium, and 10,000 people came to watch.

Our best players came from Southie: Paul Toland and Jackie Wayland. Southie High also had some terrific players, such as Gary Farina, who was a tremendous halfback. I was playing linebacker, and I think Toland scored three touchdowns.

Anyway, it's late in the game and we are winning 19-0. Our coach, Charlie McCoy, takes most of the starters out, and I stay on the field to give us some balance.

Southie is on its own 40, and there is less than a minute left in the game. In what turns out to be the last play of the game, a kid named Teddy Joyce from Southie, who had good speed, and who later worked as a court officer for a hundred years, takes a hand-off in the single wing, gets around the end, and breaks free, and now it looks like he is going to score. I'm the linebacker on the side he's lined up on, and I've got a bit of an angle, so I'm flying down, chasing him across the field. I'm thinking, I'm not going to let this guy score. I get him at the two yard line and knock him out of bounds. The clock runs out, game over, and we win, 19-0. I think, at least as far as I'm concerned, it's just another play. It has nothing to do with the win or the loss; we were going to win the game anyway. I just didn't want him to score.

When I got home, my father, who was at the game, said, "Hey, great game," and handed me $20. Now, $20 in 1953 was a lot of money. It wasn't very often, if ever, that I could claim $20 as my own.

That night, I went out to a party in Quincy at our end, Jack Fallon's, house. It was all guys. In the cellar he had a piano, and our line coach, Ted Lyons, was there, and he could really play the piano. So we were downstairs, no drinking, just singing songs, and I love to sing. Anyway, when I got home around midnight, my mother was still awake sitting in the kitchen having a cup of tea, waiting for me to come in.

I said, "Ma, Daddy gave me $20. He must have thought that I played a great game."

And she started to chuckle.

I asked her what she was laughing at. She said, "You know, most of the guys your father works with down at the waterfront are Southie guys."

I said, "Yeah, so."

She told me he had made bets that totaled $500 on BC High and he gave 13 points. "So," she said, "if that boy scores a touch-down your father loses $500."

That really shrank my ego right down to size. In addition to making the shutout saving tackle, I had played a really good game. I was all over the field and made a lot of tackles, plus we had just won the Bean Bowl, which was the City League Championship. I thought he gave me the $20 because of the game I played. But all he really cared about was the 50 bets he had made and the fact that he won his $500. That's just the way he was.

Another example of my father bruising my ego involved another football game and our furnace. When I played at BC High, in addition to playing linebacker, I was the backup tailback. In this one particular game my junior year, our all-scholastic back Paul Toland was out injured, and Coach Charlie McCoy put me in my first game in the backfield. I remember that we were playing Commerce High School in the City League. We beat them, 12-6, and I scored both touchdowns.

Now, one of my jobs at home was to make sure the coal furnace was going for the three apartments on our side of the six-decker. When I got home, I ran upstairs and yelled, "Ma, Ma, where's Daddy? I scored two touchdowns and we won the game 12-6." She told me that he was down cellar.

That should have been a signal, but I was so excited, I never even gave the furnace a thought. I ran down to the cellar and breathlessly said, "Dad, Dad, I scored two touchdowns and we beat Commerce 12-6." He gave me a stare and said, "Our furnace went out," then walked upstairs and left me standing there. I thought, so much for my two touchdowns. It brought me right back to reality. It took me about an hour to get the fire rebuilt, and when I finally came upstairs, I never said a word about the game or the touchdowns, and he never said a word about them either.

So that was my Dad; he had a huge influence on my life, especially in the way I handle things in a matter-of-fact, straightforward manner.

My Mother Olga "Dixie" Hubachek Cotter

My mother was a typical mother in those days and she was a big influence in my life. She lived a clean life. She didn't wear religion on her sleeve, but she was a very holy person, as I try to be. She went to church whenever she could and was a member of the

Sodality, and unlike me, I never heard her use any bad language. She completed two years of high school. She went to work during the Second World War at Hood Rubber in Watertown, where they made shoes and boots. During that three-year period, my mother worked every day while my unmarried aunt, Alice Deegan from Taft Street in Dorchester, who was my grandmother's sister, minded me.

Mom was very talented. She knitted sweaters and hats for just about every kid in the neighborhood. She also taught many of her friends how to knit while they sat on the front stoop. The stoop was where many of the ladies of the neighborhood congregated. It was just like a social club without walls. They'd sit on the stairs smoking cigarettes, knitting, and gossiping. My mother also loved to play Michigan rummy for pennies and bingo, and bowl with the Ladies Sodality. She was a good cook and made a lot of Polish specialties, but golumpkies, or stuffed cabbage, was her specialty.

Mom was very frugal. She taught me how to stretch a dollar and to never spend it foolishly. Every once in a while, she would say that my father made as much as our landlord, Ray Gaudet, and if he owned a house, we should be able to own a house. That obviously registered with me and my brothers, because, as I mentioned, one of the first things each of my brothers and I did when we had the opportunity was to purchase a house.

I think the best attribute I inherited from my mother was loyalty. Be true to your friends. She was a good, loyal friend not only to the neighborhood ladies, but also to the ladies from the rubber plant, and I've incorporated that into the way I conduct my life.

She was a good mother and wife and she did all that she could to provide a good home for her family. She kept the family together.

My Brothers, Donnie and Frank

I'd like to introduce my two brothers, Donnie and Frank. There's a six-and-a-half-year difference between each of us. My brother Donnie, the father of four children, who married Peggy Hobin from Dorchester, was a terrific athlete. He played football at English High as a quarterback and, in the 1960 City League Championship Game, when I was the line coach for BC High, we knocked Donnie out of the game with a concussion. All the kids on the team were saying, "Let's get Cotter's brother."

Donnie was also a really good basketball player, averaging about 18 points a game. He was six-foot-one, and could really distribute the ball. He played second base on a baseball team that included Bobby Guindon (Red Sox draftee) and, for two consecutive years, his team made it to, but lost in, the State Championship game. Donnie started at BC High but left after his sophomore year and had to repeat a year at English, which made him ineligible for his fifth year. I couldn't get him a waiver, so he went to Huntington Prep, which was on the top floor of the YMCA building. It was the top prep school league, and he played basketball for them. He was given a football and basketball scholarship to Northeastern University, and he played freshman football but, because of his grades, he was ineligible for the start of the basketball season. He left NU after one semester and went over to Boston State and became the Scholar Athlete Award-winner at Boston State College.

Donnie played basketball at Boston State for former Celtic Jim Loscutoff and stayed on afterward to help coach basketball with him. He also played baseball at State. Donnie was the best athlete in the family. He was more talented than I was. He wasn't flashy or anything but he worked his butt off.

Donnie earned his teaching degree and ended up teaching in Franklin, where he coached basketball, cross country, and, later, girls' basketball. His basketball teams were very competitive and were very tough. He later became Athletic Director at Franklin and served in that capacity for about 15 years, which was very similar to my background. Donnie was also kind of a workaholic. In the summer, he became the Recreation Director for the town of Wrentham and did that for a number of years and later became the Recreation Director for the town of Foxborough. Those jobs didn't pay a great deal, but they wanted full-time hours. They named the new recreation building in Foxborough for Donnie, in recognition for his years of service to the town.

Frank, who was 13 years younger than I, was always the big kid with all these little smaller friends. He was like their big brother, always taking care of and protecting his friends. As an adult, he remained a big guy.

Frank became a union plumber and worked on many construction jobs around the city of Boston. On one job, while he was still an apprentice, he was working on the same floor as an electrician, Tony Scott, who was also a professional middleweight fighter. Now, Tony Scott was about five-foot-eight and weighed 160 pounds. One of the electricians, who was doing work on the ceilings, yelled to Frank to bring him over something that he could stand on to get up to the ceiling. Scott had left his location, so Frank used Scott's boxes to make scaffolding for this guy to get up to the ceiling. Now, when Tony Scott comes back, and he sees that his boxes are missing, and then he sees who took them, he threw a couple of punches at Frank. As I mentioned, Frank is twice his size, but he's not a fighter, though he is as strong as a bull. Frank starts hitting the guy on the top of the head, driving his fists down on his head. Boom, boom, and he knocks him out. When Tony Scott wakes up, he asks, did the building fall down on top of me?

After that, he and Franny became good friends. Frank eventually had to give up the plumbing business because of health issues, and he's now retired, living in Dorchester.

Frank is very giving, generous, caring, and loyal to his friends and family. He's a terrific uncle to his seven and nieces and nephews, and the relationship he has with my kids is more like brothers and sisters than uncle with nephews and nieces. Frank also gave a lot of support to our father when Les was ill with Alzheimer's disease. He was his main supporter, and our entire family really appreciated all he did for him.

Leadership and Sports

My earliest recollection of myself was that I loved sports and hated school. When I was a kid, we didn't have any organized sports, no Little League, but we did have CYO at St. William's. In those days, the late '40s, most of the parishes, and there were hundreds of them, had CYO programs, and usually they had a baseball and basketball team. Again, back then, there were no cadets or juniors, there was only the intermediate level, which began when you reached the age of 16. The first uniform I ever wore was for the Magri Club, a baseball team sponsored by Johnny Magri, in the lower Park League.

I was introduced to basketball the same way its inventor James Naismith started—by using peach baskets. We used to go down to Dole's market, which was our local neighborhood market, located at the foot of the Savin Hill Bridge, and get peach baskets. We'd break out the bottoms and hang them on the fences at the Savin Hill tennis courts and play all day long.

When we played organized football, I played for the Savin Hill Iroquois. I was a running back and a linebacker, and my pal, Billy O'Shea, was the quarterback, all the time.

When O'Shea and the rest of our crew played amongst ourselves, that's when I fell in love with football. We even played in the summer. Instead of playing on a field, we used to play in the water down at Savin Hill beach, which was a short walk from my house. We'd play tackle football in the water, and the only rule was, you had to be at least knee deep, and we'd play for hours. No one ever got hurt. You also learned how to tackle and how to block. In those days, you had to keep your arms in to block. The technique was to grab your own shirt so that your hands wouldn't leave your body. When the season shifted toward fall, we'd move to the Savin Hill woods, which were right next to the tennis courts. On Saturdays, we'd play for 10 hours, all day long, losers out. What a way to learn how to play the game. It was always my favorite sport.

CHAPTER SIX

CYO, GANG RIVALRY, AND LEADERSHIP

We, the Iroquois, had kind of the Dorchester version of the Sharks versus the Jets against a local gang known as the Red Raiders. The Red Raiders were from the Dudley Street area, located just outside of Uphams Corner, off Columbia Road. We always played them in a football game at the Prairie, which was, as its namesake suggests, a dust bowl of a field located on Massachusetts Avenue, just down the street from Edward Everett Square and across the street from Victoria Diner, which is still in operation. I was a freshman at BC High at the time, and the only football equipment I had was my high school stuff, which I had to sneak out to play in weekend games. After every game against the Raiders, we always had a big gang fight. I don't know who won. It didn't matter. When you played the Red Raiders, you ended up in a fight. One day I took my girlfriend, Jackie York, to the movies at the Uphams Corner Theatre. Uphams Corner was considered no man's land between the Iroquois and the Dudley Street Red Raiders.

So, I go to the movies with Jackie, and before the movie begins, I have to go to the men's room, which was deep in the base-

ment. As I'm heading down, Jackie asks if I'll get her some popcorn. I go and take care of business, and as I'm coming up this
long set of stairs, I look up and I see five or six black and red jer-
seys. "That's Cotter! Get Cotter," they yell. I run back into the
men's room and get into the toilet, and lock the stall door, and
they're coming over the top, and I'm fighting them off, doing
the best that I can, getting hit on the top of the head. I don't
know how long it lasts but it seems like an eternity. I've got this
bloody nose and I'm bleeding all over the place.

Anyway, the usher must have called the cops. They come and
arrest the five kids. They go to grab me and I say, "Wait a minute,
I'm the innocent one. I'm the guy who got beat up." So they say,
okay, just leave. I tell them, my girlfriend is here. I get cleaned up
as best I can, but I've got blood all over my shirt. I go back to my
seat and I say to Jackie, I bumped into some Red Raiders in the
men's room, and we had a pretty good go. She looks at me and
says, "Oh, that's too bad, but where's my popcorn?"

The leader of the Raiders was a guy named "Palsy" and that's
the only name I knew him by. One day word comes back to us
that the Red Raiders are coming to Savin Hill, and they want an
ending to our feud once and for all. It's a Friday night, and we get
all the brave-hearted guys we can find. All the chickens found
something they just had to do that night. Now we're lined up on
the bridge, 60 strong. And all of a sudden—from the bridge you
look down Savin Hill Ave. toward Dorchester Ave.—and it looks
like a sea of ants coming at us. We didn't know how many, but
they certainly outnumbered us, and, of course, the yellow-dogs
say, "Screw this! I'm not staying." And once they start running,
a panic sets in, and that leaves only a dozen of us on the bridge.
I say to my right-hand man, Paulie Brennan, "Hey, Paulie, we
can't fight these guys. Let's take off and we'll come back in an
hour and a half."

We agree, and I go up on a roof and watch this swarm of Red
Raiders run through the neighborhood calling us chickens. An
hour and a half later, a dozen of us go back to the bridge, and say,

"Let's see if they come back." In the meantime, the cops have been riding through telling the Raiders to leave. Finally, a dozen or so of their diehards and a dozen or so of our diehards are left. They spot us and start walking in pairs up to the bridge. They walk in pairs because they don't want the cops to see a dozen guys walking together.

The first two guys come across the bridge. Now, this is the old bridge. It has a steel girder five feet high separating the walking traffic from the bridge, where the cars drive. It also has a railing that is about three feet high overlooking the railroad tracks. This is before the expressway was built, so there are two sets of MBTA tracks and six sets of tracks total.

We're on the side nearest the four sets of tracks. As the Red Raiders come across the bridge, we pair up; Brennan gets Palsy, and I get the guy with him. In those days, sometimes when you fought, kids would use a garrison belt, which was a leather belt with a sharpened belt buckle that you'd use like a whip. Anyway, my opponent pulls one out and hits me on the right side of my nose. Another eighth of an inch and it would have taken my eye out. He just tears the skin right off.

I hit him, and my first shot is pretty good. I get him up against the rail that keeps you from going into the street and we fight. In the meantime, Paulie Brennan is behind me fighting Palsy. At one point, I swing and miss, and break the right knuckle of my right hand on the rail. I eventually knock the guy out; at least, he hits the ground like he's knocked out. I turn around, and Brennan's got Palsy with one of his legs over the railing. Brennan's yelling, "That's it, Palsy, it's over. We're going to end this right here. You're going down over the tracks." I grab Paulie Brennan by the shoulder. He yells, "Jimmy, let me go, we gotta put an end to this." I cover him with a bear hug. I say we're not throwing Palsy over, so we just dump him by the guardrail. When you think of it now, it's funny, but it was scary at the time.

Just then a car pulls up, and my father and our first-floor tenant, George Collins, who was coming home from work and saw the fight, grab me and pull me into the car. Just as we drive off, about six cop cars arrive and arrest everybody still on the bridge. That was the end of it. We never fought them again, and for the most part, they were really good guys.

Many Faces of Leadership

I was very lucky to be influenced by some very strong personalities. In those days you had a million friends. But for leadership, my father was number one, obviously. Everybody admired my father, probably because he gave them work. He was someone who operated, as I mentioned, in a very humble way. He wasn't a headline guy; he wasn't a beat your chest type of guy. He influenced me in the way I carry myself. I was never a headline guy.

Dom Bianculli was another influence in teaching me about leadership. He led in a different kind of way. Dom sacrificed an awful lot. As the Executive Secretary of the Governor's Council, he could have been out at a cocktail party every night. He spent a lot of time away from his family, whom he dearly loved. They understood that the St. William's band was what really made him tick. Dom did it because he loved us. It was tough love, but it was truly love. He cared about us. We were like his family, and, you know, nobody in the band ever got into any real trouble. He was really proud about that, and that was how his leadership really showed.

Father Hart, more than anybody else including my father, gave me an idea of the true meaning of leadership. I was president of the CYO for a number of years and worked closely with Father Hart. We became good friends. I loved the guy. They didn't elect presidents of the CYO, they appointed them, and just like he did for the Speakers Bureau, he appointed me president. But in all honesty, I really enjoyed that, taking the leadership role. Leadership wasn't something that was anointed, it just kind of evolved, but you knew who had it. Just like when Paulie Brennan and I took on those two guys on the bridge. That was all part of it. I never stood in the back. I might get my rear kicked, but I'm stepping out there, because I'm supposed to.

CHAPTER SEVEN

PLAYING BALL
FOR BC HIGH

My parents never paid a nickel for me to go to BC High. I paid my own tuition; I think it was $180 a year.

Between the summer jobs that Dom Bianculli got us from playing in the St. William's band, and my paper route, I could earn enough money.

My father said to me, "If you're going to go to BC High, I'm not paying any tuition. You can go to English High, like I did."

I said, "Yeah, for one year, Dad."

My paper route helped out in two ways. I delivered 50 Record Americans. It also got me out of the house at night. I'd come home after football or baseball, do some homework, and I had to be up the corner at 7:45 p.m. to get the Record. I split the route with Joe Sheehan, and it would take us about an hour to deliver. But more important, it gave me the opportunity to go back up the corner and hang with the guys. My mother didn't know where I was. She thought I was doing the paper route. I'd hang for an hour on the corner with my friends, come home at 9:30, 10 o'clock, maybe do some more homework, and go to bed. That was a good deal for me. It got me out of the house; otherwise she would have never let me go out.

Bullying

Bullying is an important topic for kids in this day and age, especially regarding the practice of hazing. I remember my freshman year at BC High. We were in the old cafeteria, at least that's what they called it, at the Harrison Ave. school; it also served as the basketball court. It was really just a basement, with four poles in it, and when we played basketball, we tried to run guys into the poles.

On this particular day, we were at lunch. I don't know how many classes had lunch at the same time, but the caf was always crowded. There was a kid named McKenzie—I don't even know his first name—but he was a big heavy kid, and he was a bully. You know you couldn't miss this guy. He'd push kids out of the food line, stuff like that.

One day I say, "The heck with this. Somebody's got to do something about him." I go up and give him a shove and push him out of line.

He says, "What are you doing?"

"Well," I say, "you do this to little kids, so I'm returning the favor, and I'm doing it to you. You're a bully, and I can't stomach bullies. I'm not going to put up with that."

"Who are you?" he asks.

"My name's Cotter."

"Oh yeah, you want to do something about it?"

So we go down to the men's room. It's a big room; it probably has 40 urinals. We fight, and I beat him up pretty good, and that's the end of it, as far as I'm concerned. But, of course, we get caught. Walter Martin, a scholastic [someone studying to become a Jesuit] who goes on to be an administrator at BC High, has cafeteria duty and he grabs both of us. He has this ability to grab you somewhere behind the elbow, and when he gets you there, it drops you to the floor. He marches us up to the Dean of Discipline, Father Joe Keaney, who later becomes principal of BC High.

We were given JUG, which is the Jesuit version of detention, and Father Keaney kept you there until he felt you were repentant. The JUG acronym stands for Justice Under God. I was with him from early January until the Friday before February vacation. It had to be about six weeks. We got out of school at 2:10, and when Keaney had you, he kept you there until 4 o'clock. It was difficult, with homework, a paper route, and playing CYO basketball.

Anyway, years go by, and Joe Keaney is now the principal, and I'm either a first- or second-year teacher. One day, for some reason, I'm in his office. He never calls anybody by his first name; it is always simply, mister. We're the only two in the room.

He says to me, "Mister."

"Yes, Father?"

He asks me if I recall my freshman year when I had an altercation with a Mr. McKenzie, and he really stretches out the word altercation.

I say, "I remember it well, Father."

He says, "You spent considerable time in JUG."

I say, "Considerable, Father, about six weeks. I'll never forget it."

He says, "You were never very repentant for your actions against Mr. McKenzie."

So I say, "Father, McKenzie was a bully. I beat the crap out of the bully. He got what he deserved, and I'll never be repentant for beating up a bully." I turn and walk to the door. When I glance back at him, he's fighting to hold back a laugh. And now I know, he thinks I was right.

I wanted to tell that story at the St. Ignatius Award [Cotter was given that prestigious BC High honor in the spring of 2007) to talk about courage, but I didn't want the kids to think I was talking about my courage. I told them you can display your courage in simple ways. Go over and talk to a kid who doesn't talk to anybody because he's too shy, and invite him to your lunch table. Your friends don't want him to be there, but he needs to be with people. Things like that, take courage. The point is, you have to stand up. St. Ignatius would want you to stand up to a bully. My dad, Father Hart, and Dom Bianculli certainly taught that lesson well.

Mysterious Illness, Miraculous Recovery, and a
Big Lie, or Who Needs a Doctor's Note

Just after I finished my junior year at BC High, I came down with a case of strep throat that quickly became something much worse. Even with the strep, I was coming home late because my parents never gave me a curfew, then I was getting up early to go to work, so I wasn't getting much sleep. All of a sudden one morning I woke up, and when I tried to get out of bed, I immediately fell down. My leg was killing me. I looked down at my wrist, and my right wrist was swollen like a boxing glove, and I looked at my right knee, and it was just as big. I didn't know what it was. All I knew was that I was in excruciating pain. It was a pain that one would associate with a bad case of arthritis.

So Doc Lynch, who was the neighborhood doctor, came down to the house; that's how long ago it was, when doctors still made house calls. The Doc didn't know what was wrong with me, so he put me on aspirin and cortisone and ordered complete bed rest. I was literally laid up at home for six weeks. When Doctor Lynch finally figured out that neither the aspirin nor the cortisone was working, he sent me over to the Robert Bent Brigham Hospital, which is now the New England Baptist Hospital.

It was a hospital that specialized in rheumatic fever and arthritis. They put me in a ward with patients who ranged in age from 20 to 80. I was the youngest in the ward and for the entire month of August, I had to stay in bed. I didn't get up for anything and that included going to the bathroom. During that first week, my stomach was in such pain that I was throwing up every night. The doctors couldn't figure out what it was, and I was starting to get scared.

They took an X-ray and gave me a GI series, and it turned out that my entire stomach wall was inflamed, a reaction to the cortisone. They took me off all the medicine except for three aspirin a day. It helped, and I gradually got better and was released. To this day the doctors don't know what it was. I've always had a heart murmur, and they thought the poison from the strep throat might have traveled to my heart and left me with the equivalent of rheumatic fever. It was the same swelling and pain, but they never called it rheumatic fever.

I got out of the hospital the day before the start of school. Initially, football was out. I was captain-elect of the football team, along with Jack Furey, but Doctor Feldman, who handled me in the hospital, told me not to exercise and to come back and see him in a month. I did a little running but stayed away from practice. I told Coach McCoy that I wasn't coming back until I saw the doctor on October 8. That day, I went to the hospital to see Doctor Feldman and he stretched me left, and stretched me right, east and west, and then he said, "I don't know how much flexibility you had before you got sick, but you don't have much left. I'm afraid that if you got hit the wrong way you could end up with serious damage to your knees. So, my recommendation is that you not play football. I'm going to insist that you don't play football or any contact sport ever again."

Now, my father, who didn't want any part of the hospital, had waited for me in the car. When I returned from the exam, his first question was, "Well, what did the doctor say?" I told him, "I'm okay to play." Coach McCoy asked the same question. I told him I'm cleared to play. Nobody ever asked for a doctor's note or anything, so I played. Who says doctors know everything?

My first game back that year was against Boston Latin School, and that is how I met Frank Casey. I met him at White Stadium, at midfield for the coin toss, in the fall of 1954. He told me years later that when he took a look at me, he thought I was nuts, but he later became my line coach at BC High for more than 20 years and another of my lifelong friends.

A Private Breakfast with the Mayor of Boston

I played junior varsity football when I was a freshman in 1951 and one my freshman teammates was a kid named Ritter Hynes. Ritter was this little tailback, who also happened to be the son of

Boston Mayor John B. Hynes. I got friendly with Ritter, who lived in Saint Greg's [Gregory] parish, which was just up the street from Walsh Park in Dorchester. One Friday night, Ritter invited me to stay over, and I accepted. I'm an early riser, always have been, and when I woke up, I went downstairs to the kitchen. Ritter was still asleep, and when I went into the kitchen, sitting there at the kitchen table was the Mayor of Boston, Mayor John B. Hynes. I introduced myself. I said, "Mr. Mayor, I'm Jim Cotter, a friend of Ritter's from BC High." He told me to sit down and then he asked if I wanted any breakfast. He made some eggs and toast and we made some small talk about what it was like at BC High. He was the nicest man. I'm saying to myself, I live in a six-decker, and here I am having breakfast with the Mayor of Boston, who's treating me like a member of the gang. He really was the nicest man. It just reinforced to me that anything is possible.

CHAPTER EIGHT

THE BOSTON
COLLEGE YEARS

During my senior year in high school, the football team had a ton of injuries. I was still weak coming off my mysterious illness, and after playing two consecutive, undefeated seasons, we only won one game that year. Despite the poor record, my coach, Charlie McCoy, was able to persuade several schools I was worthy of a scholarship. After going through the recruiting process, I decided that I would attend Fordham University. We had three guys at Fordham from the two previous BC High teams; Paul Hunter was a sophomore wide receiver, starting on the varsity, and they also had Charlie Penner and Jack Wayland. Charlie McCoy took me, Jack Flanagan, and Jack Furey down to the Polo Grounds for Fordham's last game of the season against Villanova.

After the game, we went to dinner at the dining room of the Knickerbocker Brewery. I remember it was quite a room, made without a nail, all pegs, entirely of wood. Just before we left to go out for the evening, an alumnus at the dinner handed us all 20 bucks. I thought that was a big deal—the last time I had a 20, it came from my father's $500 wager. You didn't get 20 bucks too often. So off we went to Times Square.

I told McCoy to tell Fordham I'd come. In the meantime, we told Boston College and Holy Cross, I wouldn't be going. I was excited about Fordham and happy that I had reached a decision, but two weeks later, just before Christmas, Fordham dropped football. Ironically, the week we were down there, the rumor at the dinner was that Fordham's coach, a guy named Danowski, was going to be fired. His replacement was going to be an assistant coach from Army at West Point. He was their line coach, a guy by the name of Vince Lombardi. Lombardi was a member of Fordham's Seven Blocks of Granite, one of college football's legendary offensive lines, but unfortunately, it never happened.

Once Fordham dropped football, I went scrambling back to BC. I went to see Charlie McCoy, and he told me he'd see what he could do. Unfortunately, all BC had left was one tuition scholarship. With Fordham, I'd had room, board, tuition, books; now I was grasping for a tuition-only scholarship. It eventually worked out to include meals and books, but I didn't get a room until my senior year. I commuted for the first three years. I used to thumb to school and, as long as you had an armful of books, you could always get a ride.

I almost left BC before I started there. I mentioned that I've had a heart murmur ever since I was a kid, and, if the doctors were not going to allow me to play football, I was ready to leave and go down to the docks and work for my father. Remember, ever since I was a kid, I loved sports and hated school.

Anyway, it was 1955, the first day of freshman football practice. In those days, freshmen couldn't play at the varsity level. Before the freshmen could take the field, we had to get clearance from Dr. John McGillicuddy, the team doctor.

I remember there were four of us who had heart murmurs. We're sitting outside Dr. McGillicuddy's office waiting to go in to see if we'll be allowed to play. The first kid, Neil Moran, goes in and comes out: can't play. The next kid, Herbie Busch, goes in, same thing. The third kid, I forget his name, same thing. They could keep their scholarships, they just couldn't play football.

I'm the fourth guy, and I'm thinking, I'm going to be proactive. I want to play, and I'm not staying in school unless I can play. So in I go. I say, "Doc, listen, before you put that cardiogram machine on me, if you rule me out from playing football, I'm going to tell [coach Mike] Holovak, to shove his scholarship. I want to play football. I'm not too concerned about getting an education at Boston College."

He looks at me and says, "Really, we'll let me put you on the machine." He hooks me up and says, "Yeah, you've got a heart murmur."

I say, "Well, it's your call. If you tell me I can't play, you can tell Holovak to keep his scholarship. I'll go work the docks with my father."

He says, "Well, suppose I let you play. You'll have to sign a waiver so that I'm not involved if you have a heart attack."

"Where do I sign?"

So I signed the paper and he allowed me to play. The following year it was the same thing, junior year the same, senior year the same. After I signed the waiver senior year, he asked, "Are you anymore interested in an education than you were three years ago when you came in here?" I told him, "Well, since I've gone this far, Doc, I might as well get the degree," and he roared with laughter.

I played, and started, at fullback for the freshman team for coach Wally Boudreau. I also did the kicking. I had never before kicked in a game for any team, but I could always kick. We always had a kicker at BC High, but it was the only thing he did, so you didn't try to take the job away from him.

On the first day of practice, the coaches asked for kickers. Nobody jumped out, so I said I could kick, and just like that I became the place kicker. My range was inside the 10, and obviously extra points. I was the only kicker on the freshman team. I scored the first touchdown that year against Holy Cross, which we won

13-12: I also kicked the winning extra point. The next game we got beat by Boston University, which took a lot of the guys who had been going to Fordham.

Coach Mike Holovak
(September 19, 1919–January 27, 2008)

Mike Holovak ranks as one of Boston College's greatest athletes. He is a member of the National Football Foundation College Hall of Fame. In his senior year, 1943, Holovak was selected an All-America tailback and in that same year, ran for 158 yards and three touchdowns on only 10 carries in BC's 37-21 Orange Bowl loss to Alabama. His 1942 BC team was undefeated, ranked No.1 in the country, and a huge favorite in its season-ending game against arch-rival, a mediocre 4-4-1 Holy Cross team. BC had outscored its last four opponents by the combined total of 168-6, and none of the experts gave Holy Cross a chance. But in one of the more historic upsets in New England sports history, the Eagles were stunned by the Crusaders 55-12. That historic beat down forced the cancellation of BC's post-victory celebration plans at the Cocoanut Grove nightclub. It would prove to be a godsend, as a fire erupted in the ballroom there, and 492 people perished in the conflagration. The investigation into its cause would lead to sweeping changes in the fire laws in the United States. Upon his graduation, Holovak was drafted number one by the Rams of Cleveland and played three years in the NFL, two with the Chicago Bears. He went on to coach at his alma mater from 1951 to 1959, and later coached the then-Boston Patriots from 1961 to 1968.

In those days, we only had four football coaches for the entire team. My initial impression of the head coach, Mike Holovak, was that he was aloof. Everybody knew he had his boys, and everybody knew he had his doghouse. Unfortunately, if you made his doghouse list, you never got off.

I'll give you an example. In mid-season of my freshman year, the varsity had a lousy game and Holovak had the first string freshmen scrimmage the first string varsity. George Mancini and

I were the two linebackers in the scrimmage. They ran a draw play and a kid named Turk Petracka, a fullback from Rhode Island, got the ball and took just one step, before Mancini hit him a shot. Petracka's helmet went one way, the ball went the other way.

Now, Mancini is a five-foot-eleven, 185-pound linebacker from Malden High, and he and Frank Casey were the two Massachusetts All-Scholastic high school linebackers. George had a concussion the previous week and wasn't supposed to be on the field, but he knew we were going to scrimmage the varsity, and so he got dressed. Holovak also knew he was not supposed to be in. After the hit, Holovak, who initially didn't realize it was Mancini, yelled, "Now that's the way to hit." Then he realized that it was Mancini.

"What are you doing?" he screamed. "Get off this field."

Mancini ended up in Holovak's doghouse and, for four years, he never got out. But I will say this about Holovak: He knew the game of football.

The Snorter

In the late fifties, Boston College was primarily a commuter school. Most students took the green line of the MBTA to Chestnut Hill, and once their classes were over, they would take that same green line home, often to a part-time job. The college game was also quite different from the wide-open system used today; back then, most of the teams ran out of a single wing-T formation. There was very little passing, and the numerical and physical size of the teams, and coaching staff, was much smaller. The sport also had a different emphasis, Cotter recalls. He didn't see a set of weights on campus until his senior year. In those prehistoric days, most players played both offense and defense. Substitution rules were also quite restrictive, nothing like the free-wheeling, multiple substitution system employed in today's game.

Jim Cotter, the football player, was a solid, fearless teammate, who placed the emphasis on team. He wasn't going to dazzle anyone with athletic ability, but he had a great understanding of how the game was played, and he lived for the competition, and the mano-a-mano aspect of the game.

The difference between college and high school was significant. You went from having one All-Scholastic, to having a team full of All-Scholastics, but I wasn't the least bit intimidated. Once the hitting started, you'd find out right away who could play and who couldn't. I remember we had a kid by the name of Larry DeAngelis on our freshman team. Larry was a big Armenian kid from Watertown. He was a chiseled specimen and snorted and made all sorts of bizarre noises. One day, I was standing with our starting linebacker Frank Casey, and we were running through the lines, and I was watching DeAngelis, and I said, "Jeez! Look at that guy." And Frank says, "Wait till we start hitting." Sure enough, he went in the tank. He never played a minute.

The way Holovak set it up, every Monday the first string freshman would practice against third string varsity. He'd have the first team varsity just loosen up and then go in. The only time that changed was when Holovak thought they lost a game they should have won, and that happened a couple times that year. In those cases, it was first string freshmen against first team varsity, which we all loved. It gave us a barometer to measure our progress as freshmen, and we had a great freshmen team.

Unfortunately, many of those guys flunked out and never played beyond freshman year. The best of them all was a kid named Jack Geherty. He was an All-America tackle at South Boston High School. We also had two terrific tackles on the varsity football team, including John Miller who wound up playing for the Packers, and Frank Cousineau, who was a returning Korean War veteran. It was almost comical; neither one of them could block Geherty. We played a 6-2 defense, and they couldn't block Geherty, he was so quick. He'd beat the blocks and be in the backfield in a flash. Miller, the starting tackle, would be cussing walking back to the huddle—jeez, I can't block that Geherty. The kid was great, but unfortunately he flunked out along with half the team. If those guys had been able to stay in school, Boston College might have gone on to be the best football team in the east.

I lettered on the varsity my sophomore year. I played some receiver on the third team. Casey played some linebacker on the second team. When the coaches switched me from fullback to receiver, I didn't know what I was doing. But my position coach, Bill Flynn, who would go on to become the school's athletic director and was the best coach on the staff, taught me about the position. I knew my place on the team. I wasn't complaining about playing time. I also did some kicking. I didn't play a significant role, but I did enough and played enough to earn a letter.

The Team Confronts Racism in the South

In 1956, Boston wasn't exactly at the forefront of racial equality. The Red Sox were the last team in major league baseball to integrate, and the N word was casually used in everyday conversation. The color of a man's skin never mattered to Jim Cotter. He wouldn't allow anybody to be bullied because of race. He placed a priority on a player's ability to work hard for the team, regardless of skin color.

We opened the 1956 season in Miami. We played pretty well but lost 28-14. It was the worst season we had during my varsity career, and we finished with five wins and four losses. After the game, one of the Miami players, their captain, John Varoni, who was from East Boston, invited the entire team to the Miami campus for a party. We had only one black kid on the team, a fullback by the name of Larry Plenty. Larry, because of his color, couldn't leave his hotel room except to go to the game. He had all the game meals in his room. So instead of going to the party, three of us, fullback Bernie Teleszewski, and John Doherty, and I went back to the hotel, to Larry's room, with a case of beer.

Well, after a few beers, we decide to go for a swim. Larry was at first hesitant.

"I can't go," he says.

"C'mon, nobody's down there, plus it's dark out," we say.

The four of us take the service elevator down to the pool, and now we're swimming around having a great time. Meanwhile, the rest of the guys are beginning to straggle back to the hotel. I don't quite remember, but I think we had a 1:30 or 2 a.m. curfew, something like that. So the guys see us in the pool, and now they're starting to jump in. We've got Larry, this black kid, in his white underwear, swimming around, and one of the hotel workers comes out and yells some pretty racist stuff at Larry. You've got to remember this was well before the civil rights movement and, in the South in 1956, there was a considerable amount of prejudice towards blacks. Our answer to the hotel worker was—to put it in a way that is more polite than what we said— "No way!"

We continue to swim around, and now there're more hotel workers around the pool, and it looks like we're all going to get arrested. Larry's afraid he's going to be hung from the mast. Fortunately, Father Maurice Dullea, the moderator of athletics, comes out and cooler heads prevail. We get out of the pool and go back to our rooms by the service elevator and don't surface until the next afternoon.

Looking back, it was a proud moment for us as players, and a proud moment for the institution of Boston College. We didn't see any color, we were just protecting a friend and member of our team.

CHAPTER NINE

A TWO-SPORT ATHLETE

Around this time, the AFL (American Football League) was in the planning stage. The league was established with the intent of becoming a legitimate challenger to the monopoly of the more established NFL. Suddenly, "big" money started to come into the professional game, and as a result, the college style of play also changed, morphing into almost a professional training ground, or farm system, for the pro game. More coaches were added to college staffs, salaries were increased, along with the introduction of nutrition, and strength coaches. The game of college football became a 24/7, 365-day operation, but Holovak was reluctant to change with the times.

The coaching profession was different back in those days. A lot of guys didn't really know how to coach, in comparison to the way guys coach today. Today, every practice and every drill is broken down to the last second, but back then, a lot of time was wasted on the practice field. I question how good a coach Mike was. He was very set in his ways, and very stubborn. I'm not sure how much scouting they did either. In my senior year, as I mentioned, we lost three games and finished 7-3, but the loss to Clemson made me question how good his staff really was. When Holovak lost Gil Bouley, who was our line coach, that was a big

loss. Two years later, he lost Flynn, and both of them were replaced by guys who I thought were inferior coaches. Vinny St.
Pierre replaced Bouley, and he was just a kid, 24 years old. He
had been on the team, but was injured, and didn't play his junior
and senior year, and it wasn't that he was a bad coach, he was just
inexperienced.

Larry Sullivan replaced Flynn. He played at Notre Dame and
in the Canadian league. So you went from Bill Flynn, one of the
best coaches, who would kill us in conditioning drills, to Larry
Sullivan; in my opinion, there was no comparison. So I think
those things hurt Holovak. He was hampered during my four
years by not having a great staff. I'm also not sure how much he
even listened to his staff. He and Bouley had a fight and almost
came to blows, and that's when Bouley quit. But Mike was a good
man, a real good-living guy, and I respected him as a person.

Here's an example of what I mean by the scouting: I think it
was Lou Florio, the assistant line coach, who scouted Clemson.
His report said that you can't run against this team; you've got to
throw. Well, I was an end, and all the receivers agreed after the
game that they were the best defensive backs we had ever played
against. So after being down 21-6 in the first half, we came out
in the second half and ran the ball the whole second half, and they
couldn't stop us. But we still lost 34-21. So whichever coaches
scouted them did a pretty lousy job.

A Game at the 'Cuse

Senior year, in the second game of the season, we're playing at
Syracuse, at old Archbold Stadium. The Orangemen were picked
to be the best in the East that year, and we go up there, and we're
kicking their butts all over the field. They get a cheap first half
touchdown, but we're still winning 14-7 just before the half.
Don Allard, our quarterback, is having a great game and we have
time for one more play. Holovak tells us to keep it on the
ground. In the huddle, Don says, "We're not keeping it on the
ground; we're going to throw for one." I was the tight end, and

Jimmy Colclough, who later played for the Patriots, was the split wide receiver. Syracuse was really good in the secondary, so we had been hitting a lot of curl-ins and down-and-out stuff, but Allard wants to throw deep. Alan Miller, who played nine years with the Raiders as a blocking fullback, misses the block, and their guy goes right over him and hits Donny's plant leg just as he's throwing. Down goes Allard and we go off at the half, with our quarterback out, but leading 14-7. Unfortunately, we ended up losing 21-14. We lost three games that year: Syracuse, Clemson, and a game that we shouldn't have, Villanova. In those days, there were only five bowls and Syracuse went to the Orange, Clemson to the Cotton, and we went to the "Toilet Bowl."

George Larkin Oversleeps

My junior year, we were playing a game at Marquette in Milwaukee. It would be the last year they played football. Our starting center, George Larkin, overslept and missed the plane. He showed up Saturday morning and, of course, Holovak was so angry that he wouldn't play him. It really didn't matter. Marquette wasn't very good, and we beat them rather convincingly. We played the game at County Stadium, and there couldn't have been more than 6,000 people there, but their stands fanned back, so it really looked like there wasn't anybody there. After his stunt, Larkin was in the doghouse for the rest of the season.

Shortly after the season ends, Frank Casey and I are walking down to help elect a captain for next year's team, when our current senior captain, Tom Sullivan, intercepts us and asks, "Who are you going to vote for?"

I tell him Eddie DeGraw.

He says, "Forget it, George Larkin is going to be captain."

"George Larkin!" we shout in unison.

It turns out that Sullivan has it all set up.

The entire team meets in a little amphitheatre type room in the business school, getting ready to vote for the captain. Looking through a little glass window, I can see Holovak outside with the rest of the coaches. He's wearing this goofy soft cap. Tommy Sullivan hands out the ballots. Acting like nothing is rigged, we vote, and pass it down, while Sullivan is going through this charade. He's got three piles, one piled high with a lot of votes, and two smaller piles with a few votes. Sullivan counts the votes and announces George Larkin. Holovak, who has come into the room, looks up with his widened eyes, and mouths the words, "G-e-o-r-g-e L-a-r-k-i-n!" Larkin is the last guy that Holovak would have expected to be elected captain. When it's announced, George goes down and shakes hands and we give him a standing ovation. Holovak comes in with this puss on and shakes George's hand, and we go over to dinner.

George turned out to be a pretty good captain. He was a good leader and a good kid; he just overslept.

"Clean Living" and the Coed

Larry Eisenhower, who would later star for Holovak playing for the Boston Patriots, joined the varsity my senior year. He even gave me the nickname, "Clean Living." I got that because I wasn't a big partier or big drinker. Senior year, I finally had housing, and I roomed with a guy named Mike Hurley, while Larry lived down the hall. One night, Eisenhower comes down with his girlfriend and says, "Hey, Clean Living, can I hide my girlfriend in your closet?"

"Sure."

Now, the closet is simply a step, about six inches high off the floor, covered by a curtain, and I'm sure I don't have a shot of concealing her, but I'm willing to give it a try.

At 11 o'clock, Father Caulfield starts to make his rounds, and at 11:20 he gets down to our room. He looks in and says, "Hi, Jim, hi, Mike."

And Hurley says, "Hello Father, it's good to see you."

Now, Mike Hurley is a real practical joker. So he says, "Hey, Father, come in and sit, I've got to talk to you."

Caulfield is sitting about five feet away, and Hurley is busting 'em by asking all these stupid questions.

I don't know if he sees her or not, but Father never acknowl-edges the girl and leaves to finish his rounds. All of a sudden, there's a knock on the door. It's Eisenhower, and he says, "Hey thanks, Clean Living."

I must have had at least 10 fights with Larry when he was a freshman. He was like a wild stallion. He was 16, maybe just turned 17, six-five, 190, and he wasn't going to take any guff from anybody. Everyday, he was punching and fighting with somebody. I never minded fighting, so we'd fight. After all, how much can you hurt someone wearing football equipment? I al-ways liked Larry, he's a great guy. I recently saw him at a BC foot-ball game and he told me that I was always his favorite. He mentioned that one day he had a fight with John Flanagan, and Flanagan was getting the better of him. He told me I pulled Flanagan off, and gave him a couple of smacks. I don't remem-ber that at all, but Eisenhower said, "From then on, I was a Cot-ter man." Those were the good days.

The Offensive Lineman Goes Back to School

Danny Sullivan was a local kid, who played 11 years, from 1962 to 1973, as an offensive lineman with the Baltimore Colts. He was a three-sport captain at Boston Tech. One day, coach Bill Flynn sent me and Frank Casey over to the BC High vs. Arch-bishop Williams Thanksgiving game with a list of kids to scout.

BC High gets crushed something like 52-0 and we go back and tell Flynn, look, the kids on the list are all great players. But, I say, "Listen, you know Danny Sullivan is over at Boston Tech? You know his coach John Morris. Nobody's giving him a look because they've got this big Italian kid, who's the state shot put champ, and he gets all the press, but he's a terrible football player. There's no comparison between him and Danny." So Flynn says, "As soon as the season is over bring Sully down to the college."

I brought Sully down to see Father Edmund Walsh, S. J., the admissions director at Boston College. Danny had good grades at Tech, but because he was in the technical course, he didn't have the right courses. So I suggested to Father Walsh that Danny do a post-graduate year somewhere. Walsh told us that as long as he got the courses he needed, the school would accept him.

Walsh wrote down the list of courses, and Danny and I got into my father's car and drove over to Latin School to meet with the principal. He looked at Danny's transcript and the list of courses he needed and told me that he'd accept him but that he couldn't play any sports. He told us that he wasn't going to get involved in any recruiting or that kind of stuff. I told him that was fine, and that's what Sully did. The next year he came on scholarship to Boston College.

Holovak was fired after the 1959 season, which was Sully's freshman year, and when the new staff came in the following year, Art Spinney, the former Baltimore Colts all-pro offensive guard, was hired as the line coach. When Danny was a senior, Spinney recommended him to the Colts, who drafted him, and he played 11 years in the NFL.

Getting Through Boston College

Academically, BC was easier than BC High. I never had a problem. I didn't get great grades, but I didn't work very hard, either. I remember one time Father Dullea called me into his office my freshman year.

He said, "Jim, are you aware they you had to maintain a 70 average to keep your scholarship?"

"No, I didn't, Father," I said, "But what would be the problem?"

"You don't have a 70 average."

"Well," I said, "we've got the rest of the semester, and final exams. I went to BC High, Father. I'll study for the final exams and I'll kill 'em. Don't worry about me, worry about those dopes who went to public school."

So I did what I had to do, and ended up with a 73 average.

BC was a very friendly place. Most of the guys were our type of guys—city guys. We had a big Boston-born population at the school, and in those days BC was known as a commuter school. Nowadays, with better academics and a broader student population, and with more student housing, Boston kids who are commuters at BC are a distinct minority.

I started out majoring in finance, but as soon as I saw the courses, I became a marketing major. All the hot tickets were in marketing, and they all did very well in the working world. But there was no correlation between the academic ability of those guys and the success they had in their careers.

I remember my senior year, I was worried about a statistics exam for a class that was taught by Dr. O'Brien. The previous year, he had flunked our fullback Larry Plenty, who, as I mentioned, was the only black kid on the football team. Flunking that course kept him off the baseball team, which really hurt, because Larry was a major league prospect as a catcher.

I was worried about Dr. O'Brien's exam and went to see him. He was a good guy outside the classroom but a brutally tough marker. I told him I was really worried about getting through this exam. I told him about how he flunked Plenty, and how that kept him off the baseball team his senior year. At that time, I still intended to play baseball my senior year, so I had to remain eligible. He told me the exam was open book, and that if I was willing to put some time in and do a sample problem of every problem that we covered all year long, I'd be all right. He emphasized that such an exercise would take me hours upon hours, but if I did that, he said, "When you get the exam, you'll have a model problem to go on."

That's what I did, and I got an A on the exam.

At graduation, all my buddies accused me of stealing the exam, and not sharing it with them. "Cotter, you SOB, you stole the exam, and didn't share it with us."

I told every one of them what O'Brien had told me, but they were just too lazy to do it. "I'm telling you, it's right here in my notes," I said.

They said, "We don't want to see your notes. You're full of it. You couldn't possibly get an A on your own."

Cotter at the Bat

My sophomore year at BC I wanted to go out for the baseball team, so I had to go down and see Holovak and ask his permission. It could be a problem because we were going to start spring football practice right after the baseball season started.

I told him that I wanted to play baseball, but he said to me, "Look, you're here on a football scholarship. You can go out for baseball, but if we have a conflict between your practice and our practice, you come to football practice."

I said okay, but I have an early schedule. I can do my baseball between 1:30 and 4 o'clock.

"No," he said, "You have to come to spring practice."

I told him I could do both.

He said, "Are you willing to do that?"

I told him I was. I also told him that if I was starting and we had a game, he'd have to let me go to the game.

He looked over the baseball schedule and said, "Well, I can only see one or two conflicts because most of the games are on Saturday afternoons."

So we agreed. I'd practice with the baseball team in the early afternoon, then change into my pants and put on my football equipment and go out and play football from 4:30 to 6:30. That season, I started 12 of the 21 games, playing either right field or first base. And as far as I was concerned, I was the starter. Holovak had said that if I became a starter, I wouldn't have to participate in spring practice the next year.

In those days there was no such thing as off season conditioning. We didn't have a set of weights on campus until my senior year.

So I went to see Mike Holovak my junior year and said, "Coach, I'm going out for baseball; the same deal as last year."

"Wait a minute," he said.

I said, "You told me if I started, I wouldn't have to come to spring practice as a junior."

"Well," he said, "you didn't start."

"Yes I did, I started 12 of 21 games, and that's a majority. I expect I'll start more this year." Plus Eddie Pellagrini [BC's legendary baseball coach] had just been hired as coach, and I wanted to play for him. He knew the game and taught it well.

Holovak told me that if I played baseball, it could affect my chances for starting as a senior.

I said, "Coach, we made a deal, and I'm going to play, and I'm not going to come to spring practice. I hope this won't affect my playing time, but you made a deal. I'm holding my part of the bargain, you've got to hold yours," and I walked out the door.

We had a good baseball year, but we didn't have any pitching, so we won 13 and lost 8 or 9 games. Come senior year in football I figure I'm not going to get a fair shot, but as luck would have it, a kid at my position got hurt early in pre-season and was out for the entire season. In those days, the football substitution rules were quite different, and because of them, you really needed to field two full teams. So I ended up playing a lot my senior year.

The Baseball Brawl and a Brandeis Connection

It was the 1958 Boston College baseball season, I'm playing right field, and we're playing at Brandeis. I'm on deck, and on second is our six-foot-five pitcher George Gersh, who was also the captain of the BC basketball team. Peter McLaughlin singles and, as Gersh comes toward the plate, I'm signaling for him to stay up. Well, as Gersh crosses the plate, the Brandeis catcher hip checks him and he goes ass over tea kettle. When Gersh gets up, he picks up the Brandeis catcher and slams him into the ground. Both benches run out and meet at mid-field. There's a big pile out on the field, and I go running out, looking for the first blue hat [Brandeis colors] I can find. I find one in the pile and I hit him three times in the head. He looks up, and I say, "Oh cripes, it's the coach."

Well, fast forward, and now it's sometime after 1964, because I am living in Weymouth and teaching at BC High. On my way home from school, there is a huge traffic jam on the highway, so

I decide to get off and stop in Connors for a beer. Sipping on a beer, I'm looking over at a table where Ernie Roberts, the legendary Boston Globe sportswriter, who I knew, is sitting with a couple of other guys, one of whom looked familiar. Roberts notices me and invites me over to join them for a beer.

When I go over, he says, "Do you remember Foxy Flumere?"

I say, "Yeah, Foxy, I remember you when you coached baseball at Brandeis. I played for Pelly [coach Eddie Pellagrini] at BC. "Do you remember the fight we had in '58?"

"I remember it," he says.

"Do you remember getting hit in the back of the head three times?"

"Yeah, I thought somebody was hitting me on the head with a baseball bat."

"Well, that was me," I say. "It was the maroon hats against the blue hats."

"You SOB," Foxy yells.

But as a result of that beer, he told me that he'd like to get some Catholic kids into Brandeis. He told me he had a great "in" with the admissions office. He was still coach of the golf team, and asked me to send me whatever kids I had in any sport. So that year, I gave him four names and each of them got accepted and received 15 grand in financial aid. In those days, it couldn't have been more than $20,000 to go. That went on for years, until Foxy retired.

CHAPTER TEN

CAREER MAN, FAMILY MAN

In June 1959, Jim Cotter walked away from the campus of Boston College as a proud graduate, empowered by a degree in marketing. Two weeks later, he made another significant walk, down the aisle of St. William's Church, as a newly married man. Cotter married a Savin Hill girl, Ann Grace, whom he had dated during his four years at Boston College. Shortly thereafter, in early July, Cotter made another significant walk—into his local draft board—and a six-year stint into the National Guard. It was a time when America was between wars. Korea had ended some six years earlier, and the Vietnam War had to yet become part of the American conscience. It was the beginning of the New Frontier under JFK and the build up of the arms race in the Cold War with Russia. For Jim Cotter, it was a time during which he made two decisions that would greatly affect his life. He became a teacher and coach at BC High and left his beloved Savin Hill, moving to the suburb of Weymouth. The move would end up playing a significant role in his family life.

I was graduating from Boston College in June 1959 and getting married at the end of that same month, on June 27. But I also had the service hanging over my head. A friend of my father worked for B'nai B'rith, and in that position had control over some money for graduate tuitions. He asked Les if I might be interested in going to grad school. I had little interest. I just wanted to get out of there. I went down to see Holovak and I told him about the guy who has some scholarship money for me to go to grad school, but that I didn't have a job.

Holovak surprised me. He said he had a field coaching job and it was mine if I wanted it. It paid $2,000, which at the time was a lot of money. As it turned out, I didn't take it; I just didn't want to go to grad school. Plus, like I said, I had the service facing me. If I had gone to grad school, I would have been exempted from the draft, but I'd had enough of school. I went to the draft board in the middle of May, before I took final exams. I told the board that I was getting married on June 27 and the woman at the board told me I was probably going to get drafted in July. I asked if there were any alternatives. She said, "The only way is if you join the National Guard." So that's what I did. I spent six months in basic training, then five-and-a-half years in the Reserves to complete the rest of my commitment. Ten guys from Savin Hill went in together. It was a fun experience at Fort Dix in New Jersey, and I'm glad I did it.

Ann Grace grew up on Castle Rock Street, in Savin Hill. She was also in the St. William's band and was a year behind me in school. As I mentioned earlier, I dated another girl from Uphams Corner, Jackie York. I really liked her, but we broke up my junior year in high school, and Ann jumped right in. Anyway, we went together six years, two years in high school and all through my four years of college. Going together for six years was a long time. If I had it to do over again, I feel it would have been better for our relationship if we both had had more independence and dated other people. But we didn't, and we got married when I turned 22.

I had no job, no money, no car, and no apartment. I knew I was going into the service, and Ann knew she was going to be staying home so she could save some money while I was away.

She was able to get an apartment upstairs in her parent's home, which was a great house. Her parents were great to us. Nice people, they never interfered. We got married in June, had a brief honeymoon at the Cape, and two weeks later I was in the National Guard.

The Jersey Boys

The Guard was a lot of fun because of the 10 guys from Savin Hill who went in together, and we ran the company we were in. We were stationed at Fort Dix, and everybody had to get processed through what they called the reception center. Two of our guys, Mugsy Whitaker and Joe Small, decided to fake that they were deaf. I tried to get them not to do it because they were going to end up getting separated from us. But they held to their charade and took the hearing tests trying to fake a hearing deficiency. During the exam, they have a box and the guy who's supposed to be deaf is to press the button on the box when he can hear anything. They turn the volume way up. I remember Joe Small, who was watching Mugsy through the glass, saying to me, "Jim, my ears are ringing." As he's watching through the glass, he's yelling at Mugsy, "Don't you dare push that button." Anyway, their charade lasted about two weeks before they were busted and returned to regular duty, but, unfortunately, they were separated from us.

I was appointed a platoon guide by my company sergeant, and that gave me the authority to give up to 10 day passes if our company didn't have a specific detail for us. But on this particular day, we were taking a 20-mile hike with full field packs. I don't know how much the pack weighed, but it was pretty heavy, and it was a very hot, summer day. Jack Deneen, who weighed all of about 130 pounds soaking wet, said, "Jim, I can't take this, I can't do that hike today, I've got to stay behind." I said, "Well, stay and act as the barracks orderly, but make sure nobody uses our washing machine. Out of the four platoons in the company, our platoon had the only washing machine that worked, so I instructed

Jack to make sure that nobody but the guys in our platoon used the washing machine.

So off we go, and we do our hike. It's late afternoon by the time we get back to the company. All of a sudden I hear, "F-you! You're not using my washing machine!" I drop my field pack and charge down to the washing machine room. When I get there, I see this big guy who's holding Deneen over the washing machine and is about to stuff him in the thing. When I appear, I tell him, I guess you're going to have to stuff me in the washer, because you're not stuffing Deneen. The guy backed down and left without using the machine. Jack was so proud of himself. "See, see, Jim, I didn't give up the washing machine! I didn't give up the washing machine!"

After basic training, I had to settle on a job. For a couple of weeks, I worked as a substitute teacher in Boston. One day I got assigned to Southie High, and when I walked into the class, I knew a couple of the students, Paul Flynn and All-Scholastic running back Dom Gentile. But as soon as I walked in, the girls started saying, "Hey, we got a sub; isn't he cute?" So I called Dominic up to my desk and told him, "I haven't had girls in my class since I was in the eighth grade at St. William's. Can you shut these girls up?"

So Dominic turned around and started firing f-bombs. "Hey, you 'bleeping' broads, this is a good friend of mine so no 'bleeping' talking for this guy, just sit down and shut the 'bleep' up." That was my introduction to a Boston public high school. I still laugh when I think of it.

After that, I went into the insurance business for about a year, but I hated it. That's when I got word that assistant football coach Jack Flanigan was leaving BC High. I jumped on the opportunity.

I called over to Father Ambrose Mahoney, who was the principal at the time. I said, "I hear Jack is leaving."

"Yeah, he is," said Father Mahoney.

"Have you filled that position yet?"

"Not yet," Father said.

"Well, I'm very interested."

I met with Ambrose Mahoney, and I forget the other guy's name. We took a walk around BC High and I was hired.

What a day September 8, 1960, turned out to be. My first child, Grace, was born on my first day of teaching at BC High. It was impossible for me to concentrate, and, needless to say, that wasn't a very good day for teaching American history, which is what I taught during my entire teaching career at BC High.

I remember being very excited about Grace's birth, and at the same time being very nervous about going into a classroom. I was a graduate of a business school and I really didn't have any preparation or teacher training. My first reaction was, if nothing else, I've got to show them who's boss. I wanted them to realize, we don't screw with this guy. I was very honest with them. I told them I would never give them any B.S. I also told them I had just had a daughter, and I think that got me a little empathy, but my first year of teaching was really tough.

As far as teaching went, I was green as grass, especially when it came to the subject of history. Other than one elective I took at BC, I hadn't taken a history course since high school. I was one paragraph ahead of everybody for the whole first semester. But, it worked out okay; I liked history.

I soon came to realize I wasn't going to make any money with the Jesuits. My entire salary was $5,000. It broke down this way: $4,000 for teaching and another $1,000 for coaching three sports, $400 for football, $400 for basketball, and $200 for baseball. The day I started at BC High, Ted Galligan was the head football coach, Paul Hunter was the freshman football coach, and I was the JV football coach.

Never Enough Money—
A Loaded Work Schedule

When I started teaching in 1960, my schedule was such that I was almost never home. Here's an example of my week: National Guard on Monday night, classes at Boston State Tuesday and Thursday nights, as I was working toward my master's, which was

part of the deal when they hired me at BC High. I worked at the
Post Office Wednesday, Friday, and Sunday nights and had Saturday night off. I was out of the house six nights a week, and I
had a new baby. It wasn't easy.

I maintained that schedule for three years. Finally, I worked
out a deal with the National Guard, and it came about because of
my schedule at BC High. When you taught history, you were
considered an auxiliary teacher, and that meant you only taught
four days a week. I didn't teach on Monday. After the first six
months of the Guard, I got to know this captain, Dan Dell'Elce,
and he told me that he needed somebody to type. That's when I
made him an offer. I told him look, "I'm off Monday, so I can
come down and do my Guard duty in the morning," and he allowed me to do that. I did three hours every Monday morning for
the next couple of years, and, thankfully, that gave me another
night off.

There's probably one mistake I'd correct if I had it to do over
again—I wouldn't have moved to Weymouth. I think that really
did in my wife Ann. She hated it from day one. Things might have
been different if we'd stayed in Savin Hill. When we moved to
Weymouth, she started drinking more. I don't know if she would
have drunk any less if we stayed in Savin Hill, but in hindsight, I
would not have moved.

A Move from Savin Hill

Working on the docks before graduation indirectly led to my
down payment for our Weymouth home. I was working at the
waterfront to make some extra money because I was getting married two weeks after graduation. I had some time between my
final exams so I went down to the waterfront and faced my father. I worked for him for one day, and I worked a Saturday, Sunday, and Monday for a guy named Joe Comfrey, who was also a
stevedore. It was the last load of the day, and we were in the hold
working on 80-pound bales of peat moss. The hook would come
down and, with your partner, you'd put four bales at a time on the

sling. I was at the very bottom of the hold. All day long the wench had been buckling and, unbeknownst to me, on this last load it gave way. The load hit the side of the gunwales at the top of the hold and one of the bales came crashing down. When you're down in the hold and somebody yells "Run," you don't look up; you just run. I ran right into it, and it knocked me out cold.

They hoisted me out on a pallet and took me to the Carney Hospital. Thankfully, I was diagnosed with just a bad concussion. But four years later, I received a check for $1,500 from the insurance settlement. It was like manna from heaven. I didn't have a nickel in the bank. I wasn't making enough, and I couldn't save a nickel. I had two kids with a third on the way. I was working two jobs, in addition to teaching and coaching at BC High, but I still couldn't save any money.

I took the check and drove down to see Eddie Pellagrini, my baseball coach at BC, who had a real estate office in Weymouth. It was Ascension Thursday, 1963. BC High had the day off, and I had this check burning a hole in my pocket. In those days, there was a fear that the neighborhood in Savin Hill was changing, and that left me unsure about what was going to happen to real estate prices.

I would have loved to have stayed in Savin Hill all my life, but I simply couldn't afford to take the chance. I didn't even tell Ann. It was at the height of tax season, and she was working as an accountant. So I drove down by myself to see Pelly. He said, "Jimmy, I've got time to show you one house. It's a real good house. I sold it to my brother's best friend three years ago and he put on a big family room. He wants to move to a bigger place in Bellingham." I went down, saw it, and loved it. It was on a dead end street. So I just crossed out the name Jim Cotter on my check, and wrote in Ed Pellagrini Real Estate. Then I went home and told Ann I had bought a house in Weymouth. It didn't go over very well. She didn't even know where Weymouth was. She was furious, and I don't think she ever forgave me. But I thought it was the right thing to do; I did it, and I took the consequences.

CHAPTER ELEVEN

THE PIED PIPER

The house in Weymouth turned out to be a great spot for us because it was at the end of a dead end street that had a ton of kids. Every night, whenever I wasn't working a second job, I'd come home and the neighborhood kids would be waiting for me. They'd want to know when Mr. Cotter was coming out.

We'd have a game every night, either kick ball, stick ball, or whatever. I did that for 10 or 15 years, until they were all grown up. In those days, one of my second jobs was working Sunday afternoons at the Alumni Café in Quincy. They used to sell two pizzas for a buck fifty. So when my shift ended, I'd get 10 pizzas for seven-fifty, and take them back to our street. It was enough to feed the entire neighborhood. When I pulled up, all the neighborhood kids who were hanging at my fence would start shouting, "He's here. He's here."

Let me tell you about my own kids, who grew up on that dead end street in Weymouth. Grace, Kelly, and Michael were born two-and-a-half years apart. Grace and Kelly went to Notre Dame Academy in Hingham where they were both good athletes. They both played basketball; Grace played tennis and Kelly was a softball player. They were good students and both of them went to Boston College. Grace was a theology major and Kelly was a nursing student. During her last two years at BC, Grace served as an RA, dorm resident assistant, which meant her room and board were paid and that was a big help financially.

Upon graduation, Grace journeyed off to Belize in Central America and worked for a year in the Jesuit Volunteer Program. When she came home, Grace joined Kelly in Burlington, Vermont, where she earned a master's degree in administration at the University of Vermont.

Kelly studied nursing and then moved with a couple of girl-friends to Burlington, getting a job at the UVM hospital. After two years, she joined the traveling nurse program. Kelly worked two or three months in Casper, Wyoming, and then moved on to Colorado Springs. She liked it so much that she decided to stay. Kelly got a job at one of the hospitals, and it was there that she met her husband Tim. They came back here and got married, but went back out to live in Colorado.

In the meantime Grace met Bernie Regan, got married, and was living in Stoneham while working at Notre Dame Academy. After two years, Grace went to work as the director of development at Mount Alvernia, a private elementary school located near Boston College. From there, she went to Holy Cross and for three years she was the director of special events, donor relations, and parent programs. Then Grace came back to Boston and for two years was the vice-president of the Boston Public Library Foundation. Finally, she was hired by BC as the executive director of alumni, and she held that position for six years. She is currently director of advancement for the New England Province of Jesuits and very successful; as a matter of fact, she is a record-setting fundraiser for them.

Mikey graduated from Weymouth South where he played football and baseball. He went to Framingham State for one year but decided school wasn't for him. Finally, after doing some coaching for a few years, he went to work for UPS. That was probably the best thing he ever did. UPS got him focused. They run it like the Marine Corps. He was very successful, and in the three years he was there, he had two promotions to management. In the interim, he got married to Beth Corkum. He called me one day and told me that he was quitting UPS. I was dead set against it. Then he told me that when you work 16-hour days, 5 days a week, you can't have a family. I thought, you know, he's right. After he left, I had a couple of friends call me and tell me the courts were putting on a class of 30 court officers. Mikey got into that class and now he's a court officer and has really enjoyed the job.

I'm very proud of all three of my kids. They are the joys of my life, and I love them dearly, and that includes the grandchildren. They are all very good at what they do, and each of them has two kids, which means I'm a six-time grandfather. I'd like to acknowledge them. Gracie has two sons: Luke, a freshman at Bowdoin, and Bartley "Moe," a sophomore at BC High, and both are three-sport athletes. Kelly has two children: Annie, a great student and a dancer, and Matt, a terrific soccer player. Mike has two children: Casey, who's eleven, plays soccer, basketball, lacrosse and baseball, and Mikayla, who is eight, plays soccer, basketball, gymnastics, and lacrosse.

CHAPTER TWELVE

COACHING AT BC HIGH

When Cotter returned to BC High, the football team was winning, but the culture around the team was not to Cotter's liking. Head coach Ted Galligan ran an autonomous oligarchy. He had very little interaction with his two assistant coaches, Cotter and Frank Casey. But most disheartening for Cotter, the coach didn't have much interaction with the players, particularly the ones who backed up the starters. Cotter also felt that at times Galligan was abusive to the kids, and he vowed if he ever took over the program, it would be an open and inclusive operation. When he did take over, Cotter coached to his talent. He played tough defense, focused on running the ball, and controlling the clock. He never worried about wins and losses, he simply wanted to teach his players discipline and teamwork. He took the most pleasure in playing everybody, while watching them grow as players and young men.

Ted Galligan was a good coach, an old-fashioned coach. You did your group work and worked with your position players in preseason, but once the team was put together, you might as well have been invisible. The next year, Frank Casey, my pal and former BC teammate, joined the staff. During practice, we coached the linemen; but during fall teamwork, all we did was stand on the sidelines. They should have put striped shirts on us and made us officials, for all the good we were doing. It was frustrating. After all, we both played college football and we knew how the game was played. But in those days, that's the way they played it in the coaching profession.

Somewhere along the line, Galligan grew into a very mean-spirited guy. The first year I worked for him, we won the City Championship. We had a great year, great kids, and he was terrific. Two years later, he started getting real nasty. My third and fourth years with him, I wanted to punch him out. I was so angry at him so many times. He verbally mistreated the kids, and that type of verbal abuse is something I would never do, or ever tolerate from any of my assistants.

There was a rumor going around that the administration was going to fire Galligan. Perhaps they, too, had grown tired of his act. But nothing happened.

Becoming Head Coach

Now it's summer, and I'm working as camp adviser at the playground at Savin Hill, while Donnie Walsh and Mike Ananis, who were our co-captains for the 1964 season, are cutting grass at BC High. On August 1, Joe Shea calls Donnie into his office and says, "Go over and see Jim Cotter, I just fired Coach Galligan."

Now I had to scramble. I had no assistant coaches. I didn't want Paul Hunter to coach varsity. I would have preferred he continue with the freshman team, where he had done such a great job. But Paul wanted to coach varsity, so I relented.

I was really fortunate to get John Molloy to leave his assistant's job at Roxbury Latin. It was also good of their head coach to release him. After all, it was August 1 for them too.

I found Charlie Ray from Southie High to coach the freshmen. The following year, the 1965 season, Frank Casey, who had left Galligan and gone back to coach at his alma mater, Boston Latin, joined me as the line coach, and Hunter went back to coaching the freshmen. The reason I didn't want Hunter with me was simply that he had a different philosophy of coaching football. I was more of a disciplinarian, hard working, and never had a problem chewing anybody out. Paul was more of a pat-them-on-the-back guy, and I preferred my line coach to be tougher than that. Besides, as I said, Paul did a great job with the freshman football team.

The first year we went 7-2, but it could have been an undefeated season if I'd had more time. I don't care how many years you assist, you make first-year mistakes, and I made a lot of them. I might call a play that 10 years later I would never call, and that only comes from experience. When I was an assistant, I was always up in the press box, never on the field, and on the field you just see things differently. Some of the things you do the first year as head coach, years later, you say, "Why did I do those things?" You know what I mean? You waste time. It basically all comes down to one word, and that's "experience."

We had a good team and my two captains, punter and quarterback Paul Saba and defensive end Steve Ranere, both played for Harvard in the famous 29-29 tie game with Yale. We also had four kids go to Division 1 schools from that team.

Cotter's Coaching Commandments

My coaching philosophy involved three tenets: 1. Do the best you can. 2. Play as hard as you can. 3. Be in the best condition.

I used to say to the kids, "I might not out-coach anybody, and talent-wise you might not have as much talent as everybody, but nobody will out-condition us. Nobody will outwork us." And I really felt, in all the years I coached, that was the way it was. You know, we'd run the mile. People would say, "The mile! You're crazy, football players in full uniforms running the mile!" And we just didn't jog it. I timed them after practice. To this day, the backs must do 6 minutes, the ends 6:15, the tackles and centers 6:30, and the guards 6:15. If they didn't make their time, they ran some more.

I remember Tommy Joyce, who went on to become captain of Harvard's football and baseball teams, a great athlete, All-Ivy in both sports for two years. Anyway, he had big legs and huge calves. As a sophomore, he was running eight- to eight-and-a-half-minute miles.

I said to him, "Tommy, you will not start for me unless you make the time required."

He said, "Do you see my legs, Coach?"

I lived near his family in Weymouth. His father was a good friend of mine; we used to coach Little League together.

"I'm telling you, Tommy, I'm not going to start you. I cannot look these other guys in the eye, if I start you, after you're running eight-minute miles, and I start you, over them. You either make your mile time of six minutes or you don't start. Go back to Weymouth, I don't care."

By the time he was a senior, he was running 5:25 to 5:30 miles. Yeah, it was all mental. He just had to get through the barrier.

So condition-wise, we were in great shape. Nobody could out-condition us. I said that every year. No one is ever going to out-work us, or out-condition us, and, for the most part, nobody ever did.

The Cotter Philosophy

Buddy Teevens, head coach of Dartmouth College, says the best coaching in America is done at the high school level because you never know who is going to walk through that door. Part of my so-called coaching philosophy was simply working with whatever talent walked through the door.

In my first six years as head coach, we didn't have a legitimate running back, and by legitimate I mean the guy who can get you 1,000 yards today. We played a good Southie team in 1966, and on our team that year we had four future Division 1 scholarship players on the line: two went to BC, one to Holy Cross, and I forget where the other one went. In that game against Southie we gained over 300 yards on the ground and lost the game 6-0. Our backs were that bad. When I looked at the film, it showed that whatever we gained, it was what the line gave us. Wherever the backs were hit, that's where they stopped. In that game, we were stopped four or five times inside the 10, and in addition, we didn't have a quarterback. Anyway, with 30 seconds to go, Pat Flaherty returned a punt 60 yards to beat us 6-0.

Somebody once said to me, you could have won 300 games. I told him there were some years I didn't have a running back that could beat me in the 40-yard dash. We'd always get hard working, tough kids, but we went years without any great athletes. Here's what I mean: We might have a back get 60 yards in a game but only one yard on his own. He only got as much as the line gave him, but he was the best I had. I couldn't operate with the philosophy of, "I'm going to die if I don't win." That was never my philosophy. So what do I do? We grind it out, throw in some play action passes, and hope we don't get intercepted.

I believe our dearth of talent could be attributed to the perception that BC High was too tough academically. Kids were simply afraid to come to BC High. There was a feeling you couldn't go to BC High, play sports, and also survive academically. I can't tell you how many kids from Archbishop Williams, or Xaverian, or Catholic Memorial said to me, "I really wanted to go to BC High. If only I could have balanced the academics with the sports, I would have gone there in a second."

So, because of that, our general game plan was to play tough defense, run the ball, and try to control the clock. It took until guys like All-Scholastic tailback Eddie Cronin in 1970 and Leo Smith in 1977 came along before I had my first legitimate running backs.

Picking Assistant Coaches

When I hired my first assistant, John Molloy, in 1964, he was only a couple of years older than I, but he had been coaching since he was in college. He coached at Cathedral High School with Eddie Lambert, who later took over at Boston Latin, and he did that while he was still going to school at Boston University. John stayed with me for seven or eight years, only leaving when he became a vice-principal of the Mary E. Curley Junior High School and later principal of the Harrington School in Brighton.

The following year, in 1965, Frank Casey came back and stayed with me for 20-some-odd years. While John was here, Frank was the head line coach and first assistant. He handled the varsity line from tackle to tackle, while John coached everybody else.

Frank and I played against each other in high school in 1954, during our senior year. He was a starter at Latin, and his senior year we were captains of our respective teams. We both went to Boston College on scholarship and played together our freshman year. But sophomore year, Frank left school and went to work to support his family. He came back the following year, and he graduated a year after me. He ended up the captain of BC's 1959 team, which was Holovak's last year. So from 1965 on, Frank stayed with me, acting pretty much as a co-coach. It wasn't like head coach and assistant coach. He coached the defense, and I coached the offense. We stayed together until the mid-'80s. He left when his son John, who was a guard on one of the better lines I ever had, graduated and went to play at Tufts University. Frank left me so that he would be able to watch his only kid play football.

When Frank left, I hired Bobby Lynch as my line coach. Bobby did a great job and stayed with me until he was offered the head coaching job at Dedham High School. He taught at Dedham, and after he left the head coaching job, he became their athletic director, finally retiring in 2008. Now he's back at BC High, teaching and coaching the seventh and eighth grade kids.

After that, Bill Timmins came on board with me. Billy played for me when I was an assistant coach with Galligan, working as the line coach. Bill coached over at Cambridge Rindge and Latin, and I got him to come over when Bobby left for Dedham. Bill was the line coach with me for a number of years, until he went back to Cambridge to become their head coach. I was really fortunate with these guys. Then, of course, I had Jim Rourke for a couple of years. We had our differences, but he's a good coach, and, of course, Steve Trapilo was outstanding. I really lucked out, with guys like Molloy, Casey, Timmins, Lynch, Rourke, and Trapilo.

In every coach I ever hired, I always looked for a guy who, first of all, liked kids. They had to be comfortable working with kids and they had to leave their egos at home. We'd all played football. So were we out there to impress the kids with how good we were, or were we out there to coach them?

My final criterion for hiring a coach was that he had to be respected and respectful. All those guys would fit into that category. I would rather find guys who didn't know football, but had all those qualities, than the other way around. You could always teach the x's and o's.

I had a great bunch of former assistants: Arthur Bradley, Mike McGonagle, Steve Hughes, Jon Bartlett, Frank Belcher, and, at the end of my tenure, Adrian Hernandez, John Lynch, Eddie Lynch, and Mark Stonkus. All those guys were really classy. They loved BC High, and at the same time, they were real gentlemen. They checked their egos at the door, and really liked to work with kids, which was the way I wanted to operate.

Coaching Help and "Black Jack"

One guy I did lean on that first year, and did spend some time with, was Bob Margarita. Bob had been the head coach at Georgetown University when they dropped football a couple of years earlier. He came back to his native Massachusetts and worked as an assistant coach at BU for a couple of years. The year that I got the head coaching job at BC High was the same year he became the head coach at Stoneham High School.

I was introduced to him through Globe editor Gene Mack, Jr., whose father used to draw sports cartoons for the Boston Globe. Mack used to come up and drink when I was tending bar at Connors Tavern. I told him I had just been hired as head coach at BC High but that I didn't know anything about defensive secondary play. I had never played it or coached it. I was the line coach.

Mack told me about his brother-in-law, Bob Margarita. Mack called Bob. I went up to his house for two or three nights, and he x'd and o'd me to death. He was so knowledgeable.

In the secondary on defense that first year, in addition to senior Jeff Fleming, I started two sophomores, Steve Fisher and Frank Gordon, and between them, I think, they intercepted 16 passes as sophomores. They were a great addition to the team, all because of Margarita's coverage schemes.

Football was pretty simple in those days. It wasn't the wide open attack, like it is now. So, we had a simple key. We keyed the back away from the strength. I realize this might be a bit technical, but this is what we ran. If a team is in a fullback right half, and the strength is to the tight end flanker, we key the right half, which we called 'black jack." And wherever black jack went affected our coverage. Our secondary guys keyed black jack. So if the right halfback flowed to the strength, we would rotate to a three deep. If he went away from the strength, we'd rotate back. It was just a simple key, a simple rotation, and many times the quarterback never saw our free safety, Frank Gordon. He might spot the tight end running down the middle of the field, but he'd never see our defensive backs rotating into the middle, and that's how we were able to pick off so many passes.

It was great, and Bob was a great help to me. BC High and Stoneham High never played each other in a regular season game but always scrimmaged the last week before the start of the season. Bob just passed away [August, 2008], and after he retired from coaching, he stayed at Stoneham as the equipment manager, working right up until his death.

Fellow Coaches, the Relationship with Catholic Memorial

I was lucky to coach against some of the best coaches in Massachusetts, and even though we didn't always agree philosophically, we had great respect for one another. My only beef with legendary Hall of Fame coach Armand Colombo was that he ran the scores up. I didn't dislike him personally; he was a good guy, a funny guy, really a hot ticket. He was a good fellow off the field. Let me give you an example of his running up the score.

I was a first-year head coach, and in our next game we were going to play Archbishop Williams, which is where Colombo was coaching at the time before going to Brockton High, so I went up to scout them playing Malden Catholic. The coach at MC was a kid named Eddie Recupero, who had been an assistant for Armand for five years. Anyway, Archies is killing them, 35-0, with about a minute to go. When Archies recovers the ball in a fumble, Armand puts the first team in, and a kid named Joe McDonald, who would play fullback at BC, carries the ball six straight times and scores to make it 42-0. Now, if you're going to do that to your former assistant coach, then you never want to be in that situation as somebody he doesn't know.

That was the only thing I didn't like about Armand; he used his top players to run up the score, rather than fielding his bench. I talked to him a number of times about it, and his answer was always, "Why should I penalize my kids, and take them out, because the other team is lousy and not prepared? My kids deserve to play as much of the game as I want them to play." That was always his response. He didn't consider it running up the score.

Jim O'Connor, the head coach at Catholic Memorial, is one of the best coaches and just a wonderful guy. I always thought the reason we never had a post-game incident between BC High and CM was because of our close friendship. In our coaching fraternity, I honestly don't think there was anyone I disliked. I got along with everybody. You may not like some of the things they do, but by and large, they are all pretty good guys.

In the early days of the BC High versus CM rivalry—and by early, I mean the early '60s and into the '70s—it was very important to win that game. It was important for me, the players, and for the school. It became less so as the years went on, because CM's program hasn't been very good for the last 15 years.

So BC High has been dominant in the recent series. Now, BC's rival is Xaverian High School; but back in the day, the game with CM was a big deal, and it was really about bragging rights for the city. There were a lot of city kids on both teams and the games were real battles.

CHAPTER THIRTEEN

ALWAYS THE BEST

In my first 11 seasons at BC High, we never had a losing season, and what I'm equally proud of is that we never ducked anybody. When Frank and I played at Boston College, we played with a lot of kids who were All-Scholastics from the suburban schools. Many of them weren't that good, but they used to look down on the City League.

There was no way we could show them we were better because we never had the opportunity to play outside the league. That always bothered me, and I pledged that if I ever became a head coach, and had the opportunity to schedule non-league games, I would.

As it turned out, some of the City League schools had fallen on hard times, places like Brighton High, which could barely find enough players to field a team. So we began to look to the suburban schools to schedule opponents. I remember we played Saugus and Salem in the same year. I was able to pick up New Bedford in the late '60 s and Brockton in 1968 or '69. They were always a test, so we kept them on the schedule and have played them for almost 40 years.

The Mile Paybacks

It's amazing what conquering that mile time did for kids. It was such an accomplishment for big, heavy tackles to make 6:30 miles. Once they did that, they'd feel they could do anything. In the 15 years I ran in 10k road races around New England, I'd have so many of our former players tap me on the shoulder as they went by. "Hi, Coach." I'd look and it would be this big fat kid who had slimmed down and now he's a 190-pound guy, working for a living. "Hey, Coach, how ya doing? Glad you had us run those damn miles." I heard that from more kids, but I think that was really an important thing to do.

The More the Merrier

When I hired John Molloy, he was a terrific help. He was great with large numbers of kids, and I attracted large numbers. Everybody used to quit Galligan. If you weren't going to be a starter under Galligan, he wasn't going to let you play. So I almost doubled the number of kids that first year. We had 30 or 40 kids on the freshman team and another 60 kids on varsity. So we needed somebody who could handle numbers, and John Molloy was the guy. He would take 40 linemen and do something constructive with them. When Frank Casey came back we used to let Frank coach the middle five, and Molloy coach the cast of thousands. Frank would know from tackle to tackle. He might not know all their names, but he could coach the heck out of them, and Molloy would handle the rest.

Candy Sales with a Purpose

I started selling candy and Coke with my coaches because I wanted to find a way we could see every kid after practice, before he left for the day. There wasn't anyplace in school to get something to eat, so the candy and soda provided sustenance. Many of these kids were traveling an hour before they got home, and without anything to eat, they'd be starving. Once McNeice Pavillion was built, we were able to wheel out a big cooler filled with candy and tonic. All the coaches would be there, and we'd get to see every kid when they left every day. If Johnny had a bad day, after we'd chewed his butt for 20 minutes, we'd tell him to flush it and come back tomorrow. Every day, you'd see a coach walking a kid to the door, and that was the primary reason for the candy sales.

We also made about a grand a year, and with that money I could take my coaches out for dinner. I could buy them all matching clothing so that we'd look good, look like a team. Those were my reasons for doing it. I wanted each player leaving practice to have made a connection with one of the coaches.

Secret Supply Store Leads to a Sophomore Team

I first met Chetty Stone when he was working at Bucky Warren's Sporting Goods, which was a legendary establishment located on High Street in the heart of Boston, at the edge of the Financial District. It was known far and wide simply as Bucky's. Chet was one of their salesmen. When I met him, he told me my old high school coach, Charlie McCoy, who had become a priest, was his parish priest in Scituate, and that McCoy had actually baptized both him and his brother, converting them to Catholicism.

It was McCoy who got Chetty, a great athlete who was a star center fielder in the Boston Park League, the job at Bucky Warren's. After several years at Bucky's, Chet left and joined Holovak and Coughlin, another sporting goods store of local renown, that was located on the Cambridge-Arlington line. When Harvard's athletic equipment manager died suddenly, Chetty was offered the job. He stayed at Harvard for over 30 years, and became a legend in his own right.

Here's how we started the sophomore team. One day Chet mentioned that he was getting rid of some of Harvard's game pants; he asked me if I would like them. Why not? He said that they weren't exactly our colors. I told him they were close enough. If he was getting rid of them, I'll take them, and use them as practice pants. I think I got 10 years out of them.

Years after I stopped using them for practice pants, I used them as part of the new sophomore team uniform. I started the sophomore team because I hated to cut kids. I felt if anyone wanted to play high school football, he should have the opportunity, and creating the sophomore team was a perfect solution. I paid the salaries of the sophomore coaches by raffling off a pair of Patriots season tickets and, depending on the fortunes of the Pats, I'd raise between one or two grand. If I raised two, I'd hire two coaches; if I raised only a grand, I'd hire one.

Put Me In, Coach, or Football Field Fairness

We really tried to be fair to every player. We worked the kids with scrimmages and drills, making them as competitive as we could. I wanted to give every kid a fair shot to be a starter. I always explained to them the reasons that they weren't starting, and I think the kids always felt that they had a fair shake.

I told them, "I'll never B.S. you. I'll always be honest with you. I will never be dishonest with you." When I look back on the coaches I had, whether it was at BC High or at Boston College, they were all fair guys, and that's the style I tried to emulate.

Friday Night Lights

We had been talking about installing lights at our field for some time, but our school president, Father Fahey, was dead set against it. He said, "We're not going to put up any lights as long as I'm here. All it would take would be one incident with the kids from Columbia Point, and we might as well close this school down." I didn't agree with his decision, but he was probably right; the school didn't want any trouble from the neighborhood.

It took the hiring of Father Charles Kelley, S.J., and Principal Bill Kemeza, plus the overwhelming approval of the Board of Trustees led by Chairman Bob Howe, to finally put the plan for lights into action.

Once I had the approval, it sparked another great rally to the cause by my former players. I told the board that I would raise the money, and it wouldn't cost the school one cent. I told them that I'd only ask my former players, who at that time numbered 1,000, and the kids I had counseled. I talked to Bob Howe and the development director and said, "All I need is addresses and phone numbers." I got a list of names from each class and addressed every envelope myself. It took hours. I was too stupid to use one of those automated labeling machines.

I divided the list into three groups. The first group was the guys who I knew were doing very well, and I asked if they could give a $1,000. The next group I asked for $500, and everybody else $100. I told the board I asked for the money in addition to their annual giving. Ninety percent of my students responded and, in four weeks, I had raised the necessary $146,000 to install lights. Bob Howe and I were sitting with Development Director Mike Reardon, who has since left, and Bob himself wrote out a check for the lights. He slid it on the table and Mike Reardon went to grab it. I stopped him and said, "This isn't for you, this is for the lights." It was a check for $5,000. Joe Corcoran gave $5,000 and Bob Conroy gave us $10,000. Those were the biggest checks we received.

I wanted the lights to create some excitement. It was Friday night lights. Most of our kids are suburban kids, so if we had a game on Friday night, they could hang around the school, go to the game, and then go home. If we played a game on a Saturday afternoon, we couldn't draw flies. All we'd get would be the parents of the players. And with the bigger night crowd, everybody had fun.

CHAPTER FOURTEEN

STORIES FROM
THE SIDELINE

*C*oach. *It defines his life and is a word that Cotter deeply cherished during his 41-year reign at BC High. He freely admits that no amount of playing or working as an assistant coach can adequately prepare one for being the head man. You have to learn it, and he learned it well. Cotter earned his first state championship in 1977 and book-ended that championship 23 years later, with championship number two. Cotter took great satisfaction in hiring quality assistants, guys who wanted to teach kids how to play the game better, and once you worked for Jim Cotter, you became a loyal friend for life. But what comes through, clearer than a window on the Hancock Tower, is the love and deep affection Cotter has for BC High. One of his former players, Eddie Cronin, said it best, "Jim Cotter is BC High." Despite the health difficulties he has encountered, Cotter is greatly comforted by the loyalty the BC High community has shown to the man who freely gave the school so much of his soul.*

For the most part, the kids at BC High were good kids, but every so often they'd try something dumb, and I'd find out about it.

I remember we were playing Hingham in 1976, on Columbus Day weekend. We were supposed to play them on a Saturday, but it poured rain, so it was rescheduled for the Monday holiday. The kids had planned a big party for Sunday night, and even though we were now playing on Monday, they never cancelled the party. We lost the ballgame to a team we probably should have beaten pretty easily. It was a good Hingham team, but we were a better team.

Then I find out that everybody went to the party, and some of them were driving. I talked to the kids Tuesday at practice. "I want the guys who were drinking at the party to stay after practice," I told them. "We're going to have some punishment for you for not being smart enough to be ready for a game. Anybody who didn't go to the party, go to the locker room."

Most of the team stayed on the field. Everybody, Leo Smith, Joe Nash, almost the whole starting team stayed out on the field, except for two kids. They went in, and I didn't think much of it. I figured all the kids who went to the party had stayed out.

Later, Billy Brennick, who was one of our tri-captains along with Leo Smith and Joe Nash, said to me, "Coach, I've got to tell you, those two guys were at the party and they were drinking. Probably no one else is going to tell you, Coach, but I'm going to tell you."

Everyone who attended the party ran an extra mile every day for the rest of the season. But not those two guys. They walked off the field and into the locker room every day. I never said anything, but I just thought, if they're that selfish, so be it. If we ever get this published, I hope they read this, and know that Cotter knew all along.

The BC High–Boston Tech Brawl at the Arena

BC High kids were a proud bunch and always stood up for each other. Here's what I mean. One of our players, Jimmy Doyle, who was also a hockey player, was one of the most hated players in the Boston City League. We were playing Boston Tech and the winner would be crowned the City League Hockey Champion. Well, BC High wins, and while the players are shaking hands,

Doyle gets jumped and a big brawl breaks out on the ice. Now, there are about 10 kids fighting, and I'm watching from the stands to make sure no one is going to get killed.

Meanwhile, as the fans are filing out, word gets back to me that a fight has broken out in the foyer. I'm down the far end of the arena, so I go running to see if I can stop the fighting, when one of my football players, Chucky Anadore, intercepts me on the steps leading down to the foyer. He says, "Coach, don't worry, we've got it under control."

I look down, and there are two of my players, Jimmy Griffin, who was the toughest kid I ever coached, and Steve Boiardi, standing back to back, and there're blue jackets (Tech colors) lying all over the floor. Oh, the things you remember.

Friday Night Fright at Half Time

I was never a fiery, inspirationsal half-time speechmaker. I never thought those talks did much good, but on this night, I figured I'd give it a try and see what happened. I gave my "Knocked on Your Butt" speech, and I scared the kids half to death.

I forget who we were playing, but we were getting pushed around physically, and that didn't happen to us very often. I recall it wasn't a very good team, so I decided it was time for my speech.

I went into the locker room and gathered everyone together. "Did you ever have a fight, and you were fighting somebody who was a better fighter than you? And you get knocked on your butt, (and I had many times) but you can't quit. You've got to get up, even though you know you're going to get knocked on your butt again. You've got to get up, you've got to keep fighting."

And, as I'm looking around the room, I notice all the kids are staring at me wide eyed. I looked at them and now I was thinking, these guys never had a fight in their life. Walking back out to the field, one of the assistant coaches came up to me and said, "Great talk but you scared the hell out of them."

We didn't come back, and I probably did scare them to death, which is another reason why I stayed away from the fire and brimstone rhetoric and concentrated on the x's and o's. Coaches have to be motivators, but there is really no substitute for preparation.

The Most Exciting Drive of My Career

I remember the best drive we ever had like it was yesterday. It was during the 1968 season against Catholic Memorial and featured their star tackle "Big" Joe Wapple. When we were preparing to play them, we came up with a button for BC High students that said: "Topple Wapple."

My assistant coach Frank Casey and I were talking in the locker room during the week, and I said to him, "We've got to come up with something because this team can beat us." We were that close in talent.

Let's do something that takes advantage of our strengths," I said, suggesting that we put our two tackles, Chuck Anadore and Jim Griffin, side by side. Frank liked the idea. If we go with an unbalanced line, I said, they'll more than likely put Wapple on the other side.

We decided our unbalanced line would be our short yardage offense. If we were in that situation, we'd give the ball to Frank Rich, our halfback, who, even though he couldn't run five yards on his own, was one tough kid. We had Jimmy Doyle, captain of the hockey team, at fullback. So Doyle would block and Griffin would always be the inside-tackle, with Anadore on the outside because he was a little quicker. We felt we might need this alignment against Wapple because of his size. He was about six-foot-seven and a good football player.

Well, it's late in the game, and we find ourselves losing. Finally, we get the ball back on our 20 yard line, so it's now or never. I say, "Let's see if we can run the ball down the field." We didn't intend to run the ball every play, but we ran two plays and got a first down, then two more plays, and we've got another first down. Now we're on the 40 yard line. We've run it from our own 20 to their 40. Then there's a time out. Joe Amendolia, our trainer, goes out on the field with water and comes back and says, "You should hear them. They're taunting and swearing at Wapple, saying 'C'mon, Joe, we're coming right at you.'"

So from that point on, I know there's no stopping them. I say, let's just keep running it, first right, then left. Rick Murphy was the quarterback, and we must have run maybe 15 or 16 plays right down the field and scored the winning touchdown. But it was just nice to watch. Those kids came out of the huddle fast enough. They kept double teaming Wapple, and watching the perfection of it, it was like hitting a blocking sled. It was beautiful.

Paul Hunter Curses

Paul Hunter was a scholar athlete at Fordham University and lettered in four sports: football, baseball, basketball, and when the school dropped football, in swimming. He was a terrific, fun-loving guy, and next to Jim Cotter was as big a part of BC High as anyone.

We never heard Paul use a real curse word until this one particular day after football practice. Every day, after practice, one of my coaches, John Molloy, would light up a stogy, and I'd light up a cigarette. In was in the '60s, when I was still smoking.

Paul Hunter was always in a rush to get out, so he'd jump in the shower first. Molloy would get his cigar down to a snipe, put it on the corner of the wooden foot locker, and hop in the shower after Hunter. Well, Hunter is toweling off, and when he gets dried, he sits down right on Molloy's cigar. Well, all hell breaks loose, "Jesus Christ!!" screams Hunter, someone who would never even say, "Damn."

The same season, Hunter is sitting at the same foot locker, and I'm sitting on his left side. The locker across from us belongs to track coach Bill McNeil, and on the top of McNeil's locker is a starter pistol. Now, John Molloy had been a commander in the Navy, a navigator, and Hunter is an officer in the National Guard, and I was a lowly private. Well, Molloy takes the starter's pistol, points the gun at Hunter's head, and says, "I wonder if this is loaded?" Then, boom! it sounded like a cannon went off in the room. Hunter leaps off the locker and is screaming bloody murder, "Are you crazy?" and, of course, we're on the floor rolling in laughter.

The Right Guard Remedy and a Victory Kiss

I had my best comeback, and first coaching-related kiss, against Xaverian during the 1969 season. I also consider that game one of the few times our coaching changed the outcome of the game.

Like I said, we were playing Xaverian and we found ourselves down 21-0 at the half. It was Eddie Cronin's senior year, and Eddie was my first legitimate back.

Before I set up the winning play, let me give you a couple of Cronin stories:

It was the same season, 1969, and one day, our trainer Joe Amendolia came into my office and said, "I don't know what to do about Eddie."

I didn't know what he was talking about. I thought maybe he tore his knee or something worse. I asked what was wrong with him.

Joe told me he had the worst case of jock rash he'd ever seen. He said, "It looks like it's about to bleed. What should I do?"

I said, "How do I know, you're the trainer!" I told him I'd call Jack Fadden, the trainer over at Harvard, who also worked for the Red Sox.

I called Fadden, who had been our trainer when I played at Boston College, and I told him about the problem.

He told me, "Right Guard."

I said, "What?"

He repeated, "Right Guard." He said that it would clear it right up.

"Jack," I said, "that burns my underarms."

So I put Amendolia on the phone, because otherwise, he wouldn't have believed me.

The next day Amendolia comes in with a big can of Right Guard, and our captain Mike McGonagle and three other heifers hold Eddie down, spread eagle, on the trainers' table. Amendolia gets down on his knees, aims, and sprays with dead aim: "Sshssssssh."

My God, you could hear the screams all the way to Codman Square. The next day the jock rash was absolutely gone. Now Amendolia thinks he's the head surgeon of Mass General because he cured a jock rash.

Years later, Eddie, who played for Harvard, called me, looking for help. His son Bobby was at BC High and I was his counselor. Eddie told me that if Bobby was accepted at Boston College, he could go to school for free because his wife worked as a nurse in the infirmary. Eddie asked if I could help with Bobby's admission chances. I told him I'd see what I could do.

Bobby wasn't Phi Beta Kappa but he was a good enough student to handle BC, plus he's a good kid. I called John Mahoney, the director of admissions at BC, and said, "John, this is one I've gotta have, no ifs, ands, or buts about it." I told him if the kid got in, he'd be able to attend free, and they accepted him. John Mahoney is a really good guy.

Okay, now let me go back, and set up the game's winning play against Xaverian. In my first couple of years coaching, during preseason, we'd always scrimmage Stoneham. As I mentioned, it was Bob Margarita, Stoneham's coach, who taught me everything about secondary play. Anyway, whenever we scrimmaged Stoneham, they used to run a reverse against us off a power formation, and when they ran that play in scrimmage, we could never stop it.

One year, I asked him to diagram that play for me. He did, and we put it in our play book, naming it the Stoneham Special. Okay, back to that comeback game. I probably gave my best pep talk at half time. I talked about individual pride, not team pride, individual pride. I told them, look at the guy across from you, even if he's better than you, you play your heart out, kind of like a "knocked on your butt" version of things, just keep getting back up. I thought it was pretty good, and the kids certainly bought it.

We went back on the field for the second half and were a completely different team. We came out and drove the field for a score, then drove it again, and drove it a third time. The kids were playing inspired ball. Now we've closed it to 21-20, with very little time left on the clock. So, I called the Stoneham Special for the two point conversion. We practiced it every day but never ran it in a game.

Here's how it works. You operate out of the power I position; the key to its success is the back, in this case our All-Scholastic Eddie Cronin. It's a choreographed series of moves in which the fullback blocks the left end for two counts, then lets him go to the outside, and when he does, he peels back around and blocks him. Cronin takes the right half position wide right, directly behind the tackle. He takes two steps to his right, then peels back behind the quarterback. It's not a handoff, but a pitch to the right halfback, going left. The quarterback takes his normal five step drop, like he's going to throw, then three-quarter pivots around, and pitches to the halfback, who at this point in the play is directly behind him. The defensive end sees this and thinks he's got a free play. Just before he's going to cream him, the fullback cuts him. It's a great play, a great play. And in this case, it worked to perfection.

Eddie got the ball, strolled into the end zone, and we won 22-21. It was the best victory I ever had. We coached that team to win. I really felt we, the coaches, contributed to the win. It was so exciting that Father Frank Belcher, who had just returned from a mission in Iraq, kissed me on the lips, and at the time I didn't even know who the hell he was.

The Best Move I Ever Made

In 1970, I almost left BC High for another job. I wasn't searching for work, but I got a call out of the blue from Don Burgess, who in addition to being a teacher and coach at Boston Tech was also the chairman of the Milton School Committee. Milton's football coach, Tommy Brennan, was leaving his coaching position to become a guidance counselor at Milton High School. In those days you couldn't do both, which was the dumbest rule. Anyway, Donny called me and said he'd like me to take the Milton football job. He asked if I'd consider applying.

I told him I would, but I also told him that I had already signed my teaching contract at BC High and that if I were going to consider this job, I'd have to tell my boss. So, I went over to see Fr. McGovern and told him that, even though I'd signed my contract, I at least owed it to myself to look at this other job in Milton. He said before I did anything, to make sure that I talked to him about it.

I interviewed for the Milton job, and Donny called me afterward and told me they were going to offer me the job. He asked if I was serious about it. I told him I thought I was, because I didn't see myself teaching history for the rest of my life and that at some point, I'd like to be a guidance counselor. I was basically doing the job anyway. I was placing a lot of our BC High athletes into colleges, because nobody in guidance was doing much for them.

Milton made me an offer on a Thursday. I told them to give me until Monday to make a decision. On Friday, I went to school and made an appointment to see Father McGovern. I told him that the Milton job had been offered to me, and that I was considering it. He asked me why I wanted to leave BC High.

I told him I really didn't but that I always wanted to be a guidance counselor. I already did the college placement for my athletes, I explained, as well as for a lot of the other athletes in the school. They all came to me. I also told him that the two Jesuits we had in guidance at the time didn't do anything for the athletes. So he told me if I got certified as a guidance counselor that he would give me a counselor's job.

I was already certified, I told him. I already had a degree in counseling; in fact, I was certified as a director of counseling. I'm thinking, what more can I do?

I don't quite remember how the chain of events evolved, but he must have called me over the weekend. He said, "I'll give you a half-time counselor position next year," he said, "and the following year, you'll be a fulltime counselor." He asked me how that sounded. It sounded great, and I told him I'd take it. "What are you going to do about the other school?" he said. I'll tell them that I'm not going to take the job.

Burgess was really mad. They thought I used them to get a guidance job.

That decision was the best move that I ever made. Had I left BC High, my legacy would have been very different.

Alice Cotter Benson, Mom Dixie with son Jim, about 8 months old.

Dad Les Cotter and Jim as a baby on the back porch of their Savin Hill Avenue house.

Sign of things to come: Cotter the Fighter, age 5.

(l-r) Bob Peecha, Jim in overalls, and lifelong friend Tom Benson.

(clockwise from top left) Brother Donnie, dad Les, mother Dixie, and brother Fran.

Cotter the musician with clarinet and in uniform as a proud member of St. William's Band.

Cotter with band director Dom Bianculli and Father Hart as St. William's Band prepares to board an American World Airways flight to Miami, Florida, for a competition.

1954 football season BC High coach Charlie McCoy flanked by co-captains Jim Cotter #10 and Jack Furey #11.

Jim Cotter as a BC High baseball outfielder, 1953.

The old stevedore Les Cotter.

Jim Cotter flanked by Bill O'Shea (left) and Jack Furey at the 1955 retirement dinner for South Boston High School football coach Steve White. The football captains from all over the city attended the event at the legendary South Boston Blinstrubs Night Club.

Jim and Ann at the BC High prom, spring 1955.

Ann Grace at her 1956 Monsignor Ryan Memorial High School graduation.

The 1958 CYO Junior basketball champions, a.k.a. The Coal Bin Team: (Front row, l-r) Danny Ryan, Donie Cotter (Jim's brother), Mike Donovan, Teddy Glynn, Gabe Tuffo, and Mike Dwyer. (Second row, l-r) Jim Cotter, Frank Comerford, Bobby Manning, Eddie Costello, Bobby Sullivan, Jack Hutchinson, and Father Peter Hart.

Do-Wop at Savin Hill Talent Show 1953: (l-r) Kevin Joyce, Bob Lund-bohn, Paul "Wimpy" McDonough, and Jim Cotter.

St. William's Minstrel Show: Jim Cotter (second from left) with "Wimpy" McDonough (left) Danny Sullivan (right) and the Lyons brothers.

An illustrated newspaper feature about Boston College dual sport athlete Jim Cotter.

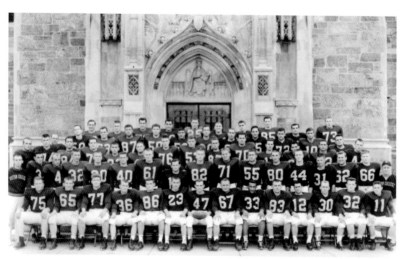

1957 Boston College football team, Jim Cotter #80, Frank Casey #60.

Boston College football starters, Frank Casey (bottom row, third from left) and Cotter (far left).

Jim Cotter graduates from Boston College, 1959.

Jim and Ann with their wedding party, June 1959.

Cotter in the National Guard (fourth row, third from right), Jack Deneen is fourth from right.

Coach Cotter with his first BC High captains Steve Raniere #35 and Paul Saba #83 (both of whom later played in the legendary 1968 Harvard beats Yale 29-29 game).

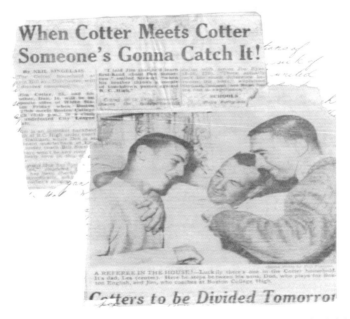

1960 newspaper photo of (l-r) Donnie Cotter, football captain of English High School; father Les, acting as boxing referee; and BC High coach Jim Cotter.

Grace as a two-year-old on the family couch wearing Mom's glasses and showing early school loyalty with a BC High yearbook on her lap.

Coach Cotter and his last junior varsity baseball team.

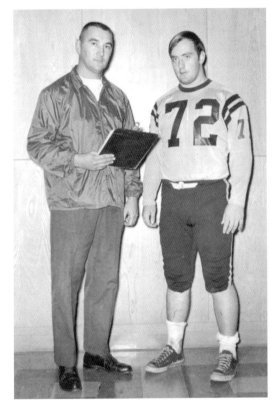

Coach Cotter with Jim Griffin, the player he considers the "toughest" he ever coached, 1968.

Dusty football scrimmage in the late '60's with notorious, long-since-replaced Columbia Point in the background.

Coach with quarterback Steve Fulchino, 1970 season.

Questionable call. Notice official on left laughing hysterically, while Cotter gives the business to referee Al Sheehan.

All-Scholastic tailback Leo Smith #24 tumbles upside down. Cotter considers Smith his all-time "best" player.

(l-r) Son Mike Cotter with Bill Brennick and John Hanlon, 1977 Super Bowl champions.

Ann, Coach, Grace, Mike, and Les at Elton Street apartment.

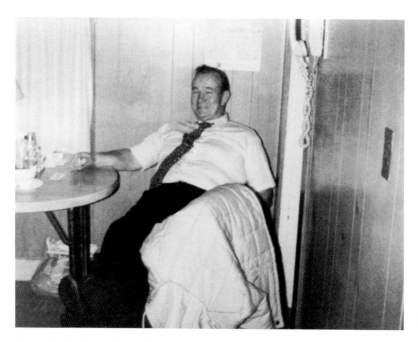

Les at the kitchen table on Elton Street.

THE 1977 B.C. HIGH SUPERBOWL TEAM

SENIORS
Tri Captain
Brennick, William
Nash, Joseph
Smith, Leo

Buccella, William
DiMino, Mark
Dolan, Joseph
Duggan, Christopher
Ferrara, Peter
Flaherty, Paul
Goggin, John
Hanley, James
Joyce, James
Lavezzo, Joseph
Loughran, Bernard
Lynch, Edward
Mattaliano, Paul
Molloy, John
O'Brien, Thomas
Penella, Joseph
Pickette, Thomas
Schiffmann, John
Smyth, Peter
Taracevicz, Stephen

JUNIORS
Bernasconi, Jay
Buckley, Philip
Campbell, William
Carey, Thomas
Casey, James
Clasby, Robert
Corcoran, Robert
Curtis, David
Dolan, Peter
Hart, John
Hogan, Terrence
Murphy, William
Najjar, John
O'Riordan, James
Pickette, Timothy
Rourke, Mark
Shaughnessey, Michael
Shields, John
Simonelli, Arthur
Waldron, Brian
Yetman, Peter

SOPHOMORES
Barry, Daniel
Doherty, William
Fitzgerald, Robert

Forbes, Peter
Hanlon, John
Herrington, Wilbur
Joyce, Daniel
Sheehan, Thomas
Smart, Michael

CHEERLEADERS
Co-Captains
Jane Lopes
Roseann White
Eagle
Grace Cotter
Cheerleaders
Janice Hayes
Anita Horne
Julie Malone
Carol McDermott
Claire McDermott
Erin McLaughlin
Rita McNulty
Ann Pellegrini
Kristen Shannon
Sue Wattendorf

COACHES
Head Coach   Jim Cotter
Defensive Line   Frank Casey
Offensive Line   Bob Lynch
Secondary   Mike McGonagle
Junior Varsity   Joe Marani
Trainer   Steve Hughes
Ballboys   Michael Cotter   John Casey

President   Raymond Callahan, S.J.
Principal   Rev. Thomas Gibbons, S.J.
Athletic Director Rev. William Mulligan, S.J.

This program was prepared and published by
1st american BANK FOR SAVINGS

**A salute to the 1977
Division II
High School Superbowl Champions
B.C. High Football Team**

March 3, 1978
Stadium Club
Schaefer Stadium
Foxboro, Massachusetts

1977 Super Bowl roster.

Elation over 1977 Thanksgiving last minute 7–6 victory over Catholic Memorial sending Cotter and the BC High Eagles to the superbowl. Game held at Alumni Stadium at Boston College.

Championship shake at Thanksgiving Victory.

Championship hug while son Mike looks on with glee.

Jim and Agnes on their wedding day.

Top row (l-r) Fr. McKenna, SJ, Fr. Jim Kane, SJ, Tim Hayes, Coach Cotter, Paul Hunter, bottom row (l-r) Mike Ananis, Joe Amendolia, Arthur Bradley.

Coaches Steve Trapillo, Bill O'Shea, Jon Bartlett, Tom Benson, and Jim Cotter.

Coach Cotter walks between his captains from the past 41 years at his last football game as BC High head coach, Thanksgiving Eve, 2004.

Cotter watching action of final BC High game at Boston College Alumni Stadium, Thanksgiving 2004.

Coach watches final minutes of final game as BC High head coach.

Players give helmet salute to Coach for the last time. Coach Mark Stonkus to right.

Daughter Grace and Coach at his last game.

Wife Agnes and Jim at a Savin Hill reunion.

Agnes and Cotter at grandson Luke's football game at Thayer Academy.

Coach Cotter with Agnes and children Grace, Kelly, and Michael, their kids, and friends after final football game.

Coach with (l-r) BC High athletic director and head football coach Jon Bartlett, Brendan Sullivan, and Sean Foley.

Agnes, Coach, Grace, brother Don, and Cotter family at 2006 Cotter Field dedication.

"Space Cowboys" (l-r) Tom Benson, Ken Halloran, Bobby Dunn, and Billy O'Shea with Coach at grandson Bartley "Moe" Regan's freshman football game.

The Marathoners and their dads (back row, l-r) Arthur Bradley, Mr. Bradley, Steve Hughes (BC High principal), Jack Deenen, and Jim Cotter; (front row, l-r) Mr. Deenen and Les Cotter.

Three generations: Papa Cotter, Grace, and Luke Regan at Luke's football game, St. Sebastian's vs. Thayer Academy, October 2008.

2007 St. Ignatius Award. (l-r) William Kemeza, president of BC High; Grace Cotter Regan, Coach Cotter, and Principal Steve Hughes.

BC Athletic Hall of Fame Donlon Award recipient. Clockwise from top l-r, Mike, Grace, Jim, Agnes.

The Cotters (l-r): Kelly, Grace, Mike, Agnes, and Coach at Mike Benson's wedding in Chicago.

Moe and Papa.

Coach Papa and grandkids (l-r) Moe, Luke, Casey, Matthew, and Annie.

Cotter's lifelong friend and former assistant coach Frank Casey with Cotter's grandson Luke.

Cotter clan at St. Ignatius Award ceremony.

Agnes and Coach at his retirement from teaching at BC High, 2001.

Coach and Cardinal Sean O'Malley at Cotter's home in Quincy, Christmas 2008.

Agnes and Jim at the 25th anniversary party.

Kelly, Mike, Grace, Agnes, and Coach at the 25th anniversary.

Dad and Grace at 25th the anniversary.

CHAPTER FIFTEEN

CHAMPIONSHIP SEASONS

Eddie Connors indirectly played a role in steering me toward a teaching career. He was the owner of Connors Tavern and the Bulldog Lounge, both of which are long gone. They were located on Savin Hill Avenue, just steps from the Savin Hill T station. Connors was a low-level gangster who came to an early, and brutal, demise in a phone booth on Morrissey Boulevard. In 1975, he was machine-gunned down, allegedly, by some of Whitey Bulger's crew. I was 24 years old, teaching at BC High, and working part time behind the bar of Connors Tavern, a neighborhood pub that drew an eclectic crowd. On any night, we served reporters or pressmen from the Boston Globe, local athletes, softball players, and anyone else from the neighborhood who, having turned the magic age of 18, was now eligible to legally purchase their first drink in a licensed establishment.

One night I got a call from a friend, Joe Clark, a softball teammate, who was a couple of years older than I. He said Timmy Melven was selling Joyce and Keane's, which was a spaghetti-thin barroom located right across the street from Connors on Savin Hill Avenue. He asked me if I'd be interested in going in as a partner with him. "How much?" I asked. He told me $7,500; $3,750 each. I didn't have any money, but I knew I could raise that much. I told him I was interested but I had to check with Eddie first.

The next night, I was working my Friday shift when Connors came in. I asked him if I could speak to him in the back room. I told Eddie that Joe Clark and I had a chance to buy Joyce and Keane's. Eddie asked about the price. I told him $7,500.

He said, "Gee, that's a good price," but then he said, "Let me tell ya, you're my friend, but I want you to know, I'll torch it if you buy it. You'll take all the young guys across the street."

I said, "Torch it, really?"

"Yeah," he said. "I don't want you to get mad at me, because you're my friend, but that's what's going to happen."

As soon as my shift ended, I called Joe. I told him that Eddie's going to torch us if we buy the place, so needless to say, I'm not buying.

Connors eventually bought Joyce and Keane's as well as the Chinese laundry run by the Soo family (who answered to the nickname of 'Murph,' but that's another story) and the beauty parlor next door. Once he owned them, he knocked through the walls and opened another neighborhood legend: the Bulldog Lounge. On Sunday afternoons, Bulldog's became the winter home of Elvis impersonator Golden Joe Baker, and he packed the place.

College Coaching Dreams

My ultimate goal in my early years at BC High was to become a college head coach. I thought seriously about moving into college coaching several times. I looked twice at assistant coaching jobs at Boston College and once at Brown University. The first time I looked at BC, Joe Yukica was the coach. There was an opening because Billy Bowes, who was their offensive line coach, had just been named the head coach of UNH.

I was probably more suited to be an end, or backfield coach, than a line coach but Yukica still offered me a job. He and I were good friends because of my work at the New England Football Camp in Wolfeboro, New Hampshire. It was a summer camp that gave me a boatload of college connections, since it was a who's who of New England college football coaches.

I was one of the few high school coaches employed there, and I worked with guys like John Anderson, who became head coach at Brown; Bob Casciola, head coach at Princeton; Joe Yukica at BC; Jake Crouthamel at Dartmouth; Jim Root at William and Mary; Rocky Carzo at Tufts; Bill Bowes at UNH; and Jack Bicknell, who eventually became head coach at BC

I was very interested in BC, but when the discussion turned to salary, it was a deal-breaker. I knew Bill Bowes was the highest paid assistant on the staff, and he was making $14,500. When I asked Joe if I'd make the same $14,500, he told me in no uncertain terms that, because I was the new guy, I would be making $11,500. I told Joe I couldn't pay my bills at that salary, but the salary itself wasn't surprising. After all, BC is a Jesuit school, and I was very familiar with the Jesuits, who can be very tight with the bucks. The money was the chief reason that I didn't take the BC job.

The Brown offer came a few years later. John Anderson left Middlebury to go to Brown, and he took Andy Talley with him. Andy became the Brown freshman coach and now he's the head man at Villanova. So I interviewed with John, who was another guy from the New Hampshire camp, for either the backfield or head freshman job. I didn't interview specifically for either one, I just interviewed for a job. As it turned out, I could have had either one. I considered Brown because I could have moved my family to Foxborough and still coached in Providence. That would have worked out well for me because my brother Donnie had just moved to Franklin, and we would have been practically neighbors.

Anyway, in the course of the conversation, I asked John about my recruiting territory. He told me my primary territory would be Massachusetts. He said they wanted coaches to primarily cover the area where they live. Then he threw in the deal-breaker. He told me that my secondary areas would be Oklahoma and Texas. I laughed in disbelief. I said John, "Who is going to go to Brown from Oklahoma and Texas?" He said, "I don't know, but they just opened up my recruiting budget to give me enough money to put somebody out there."

So I asked for an estimate of how long at a stretch I would be out there. He told me about 10 weeks. It broke down this way: six to eight weeks in winter, during the height of the recruiting season, and another two to three weeks in the spring, recruiting juniors.

I asked, "Do you fly me home every weekend?"

"Oh no, once you're out there you stay out there."

Jeez, I could picture myself on the panhandle of Texas on a Saturday night, riding an iron horse, and wearing a 10 gallon hat. It was simply too much time away from my family. So, I had to say no.

Later, I got an offer from BC, which was very intriguing. It would have been on the staff of Jack Bicknell, but once again the holdup was the money.

Even though my goal of college coaching never materialized, I have absolutely no regrets. When I look at the time these college coaches spend on the job, bunkered in the office until 10 or 11 at night, and coming back in at 7 in the morning, I don't know how any of them have a life outside of football.

One Championship, Then Another

In 1977, I knew BC High was going to be good. We had the best back in the state, Leo Smith. As I said before, we never had great backs, and Leo was by far the best. We had two great tackles, Joe Nash and Bobby Clasby, who both went on to play in the pros, plus linebackers Jack Shields and Billy Brennick, so all the pieces were in place as long as we stayed healthy. If we stayed healthy, we were going to be good, very good.

We get to St John's undefeated, but they are a good team and very well coached. They jump out to a 20-0 lead and, at one point, it gets to be 32-14.

At halftime, I give our guys a real butt chewing. I don't remember what I said, but I do a lot of yelling. We come out in the second half, and now we're a completely different team. Even though they've shut Leo down, our wideout Jackie Hart plays a key role for us. Our quarterback, Joe Lavezzo, starts hitting some passes and Hart makes some great catches, and now we've closed the gap all the way to 32-26. We miss the extra point; there's only a short time, left but at least we've got the ball. In a crucial fourth down situation, with the entire game, and certainly our Super Bowl chances, on the line, we run a hook and ladder play to Jackie, and it works, although it never worked in practice. We keep the drive going. We're on the 15 yard line with 30 or so seconds left, and Jackie makes a great catch in the end zone for the tying touchdown. We miss the extra point and the game ends in a 32-32 tie.

It is a great comeback, but we all think the tie will prevent us from going to the Super Bowl.

It doesn't get any easier in our next, and last, game of the season against our traditional rival, Catholic Memorial. We beat them 7-6, but not without a lot of controversy. Tommy Heinsohn's kid is a wideout for CM, and he catches a pass on the 10 yard line during the final seconds of the game. He continues to drive to about the 5, trying to get out of bounds, and our kids are trying to keep him in bounds. Lucky for us, it turns out to be the last play of the game. There is a lot of discussion as to whether he did or didn't get out of bounds. Ultimately, it goes in our favor, as the clock runs out with CM on the 4 yard line. Obviously, a chip shot field goal would have won the game and they had a good field goal kicker.

In the Super Bowl against Dartmouth High School, Leo Smith got hurt so we ran sweeps with his backup Jim Casey, who was a very, very good back. With four minutes left, in a close game, we ran from our own 20 and Casey carried the ball about eight straight times. We simply pitched the ball running sweeps up the field staying in bounds to kill the clock and we won our first championship, 13-6.

The next year, we could have been just as good, but we were hit by injuries. Jim Casey hurt his knee and didn't play. Bobby Clasby got clipped in the Hingham game and tore his ACL and was out for the year; he was the best tackle in the state. Then Jack Shields got hurt in the fourth game of the season and missed five games, and so it went. As I said, you have to be lucky to stay healthy.

Reaction to the Title

I look at it this way: We finally had enough talent to get there. In the previous years, we were always missing one piece, be it running back, or quarterback, the skilled kid. And even with all the talent on that team, with all the pieces in place, we still almost didn't get there. We could have easily lost two games that year, to either St. John's or CM. I remember Grace, my daughter, was the Eagle mascot that championship day, and my son Mike was the ball boy, so to have them there with me was special.

Here we are, 30 years later, and we're inducting that entire team this year into the BC High Hall of Fame. In addition to the players and the coaches, both Gracie and Mike will be getting plaques. It was a great season, and one I'll always treasure.

A Nephew to the Rescue

In the 2000 season, we had another struggle with Xaverian. They were probably a better team than we were, but our kids played great, and we outplayed them throughout the entire game. We scored a touchdown to take the lead with about a minute and a half left on the clock. They got the ball on the 20 and their quarterback threw a simple pop pass to the youngest of the Hasselbecks, who briefly played at BC. He caught it, took a step inside—the field was kind of sloppy that day—and our safety Justin Kelley went for the fake, slipped, and Hasslebeck went 80 yards for the touchdown.

Now, here's where we got our big break, thanks to my nephew, Donnie. Xaverian converted the extra point on another pass to Hasslebeck, and that gave them the lead with less than a minute left in the game. But when he scored, Hassleback took the ball and spiked it over the goal post. Donnie Cotter, who was watching from the sidelines, started yelling at the official, Don January, who was the chairman of officials for the Catholic Conference, "Hey, that's a penalty! That's a penalty! He can't spike the ball." January must have thought about it, because long after the play was over, he decided to throw the flag.

It was a 15-yard penalty, and it was assessed on the kickoff, so instead of them kicking from the 40, they kicked from the 25. We run it back to their 43 yard line. Our first play was a sprint out pass to the right, as the clock showed under a minute left in the game. The open side of the field was to the right. Our quarterback Mike Conroy, who would later sign a baseball contract with the Cleveland Indians, sprinted to the right and when he threw it, he was almost over the line of scrimmage—it was that close. Myles Staunton was running a streak pattern, and Conroy threw the ball 57 yards in the air. I'll never forget it, it was almost surreal. The ball seemed like it was floating up in the air forever, and then it seemed like it took forever, to come down. It was almost like the Phalen/Flutie pass, and for us, it was just as important. Anyway, when it finally came down, our wideout Myles Staunton caught the ball and fell into the end zone for the touchdown. What a finish! Our kids and fans charged the field. It was my most exciting victory.

During the 1999 season, we went 11-0 then lost in the Super Bowl to Barnstable High School. I knew the 2000 team was going to be good. We had a great nucleus coming back. Some of the key guys were Tim Bulman at tackle, Tim Feeney at linebacker, All-Scholastic Mike Conroy at quarterback, and receiver Myles Staunton. Although I thought the team the year before was better, we knew we were going to be good, and we were. I don't think we had any real tough games. Maybe Bishop Feehan, Xaverian, and St. John's Prep were reasonably close, but we creamed Catholic Memorial and our only loss was to Malden Catholic, and that was because it was a crazy day. Here's what happened.

It was on our home field, and the wind was howling, and in conditions like that, you're always worried because the weather is a real neutralizer. Regardless of the weather, Malden Catholic was pretty tough. They had the ability to play us physically, and in those conditions nobody could throw the ball and the kicking game was a nightmare. It was late in the game, and we were up less than a touchdown. It was a third down play around midfield, and we called a screen pass. For some reason, our quarterback Steve McDonald (I pulled Conroy earlier in the game) started running to his left and he threw the ball into the middle of the pack. It was supposed to be a screen pass outside, and one of their big tackles caught the ball and took it in for a touchdown and we lost the game.

I was furious because, at the very least, we should have been able to run the ball. So, on Monday we had a meeting. I told them that we were going to have some changes. I moved Conroy from quarterback to receiver. I don't know what it was with Conroy; all of a sudden, he couldn't throw the ball. Maybe it was something in his head. The changes clicked, and we didn't lose another game and killed Durfee High School in the Super bowl, 35-0.

The play that stands out from that season, and one I'll always remember, involved Tim Bulman. He split a double team and had one hand on the quarterback as he was trying to hand the ball off, and the other hand on the tailback, and everyone ended in one big pile. It was one of the most fantastic plays, and I must have run it 100 times. He was a beast, a great, great, player, who went on to be a four-year starter at BC, then he played in the pros with Houston.

In retrospect, the season was kind of a cruise; but you're still never sure of anything when you've got a veteran team. You're always worrying about someone having a fat head, and I was always barking at them. I think we ran our regular season winning streak to something like 18 in a row, and that loss to Malden Catholic was a blow. I never cared about records, but it would have been nice to get it up into the twenties once you're involved in it.

Enjoying the Second Championship

Cotter's first wife Ann died of alcoholism in 1983 at the age of 44
and he was happily remarried by this time, 2000, to Agnes Donahue.

Unlike my first championship, where my home life was a mess,
I was really able to enjoy this one. The difference was night and
day. It was great. All my kids were grown, so I was able to enjoy
the games as well as the post-game festivities. We had the lights
by then, and on Friday nights, if my wife Agnes came to watch,
we'd go to Sonny's Restaurant and close the place, and if she did-
n't come, I'd go to the Eire Pub. That was the special part of it.

I remember I had an open date on our football schedule and
we decided to schedule my brother Donnie's team, at Foxboro
High School. His two sons, my twin nephews, were on the team,
and it was a once-in-a-lifetime opportunity to play against them.
Danny was the quarterback and Donnie Jr. was the tight end.
During the game, Danny threw for two touchdown passes to
Donnie, but both were called back because of holding penalties,
and young Donnie was furious at the lineman who did the holding. He wanted so much to throw a pair of touchdown passes to
his brother against his Uncle Jim's team. We weren't very talented
that year, and we ended up losing by a score. After the game, I
went back to Donnie's house with the game film, and the whole
Foxborough team—well, at least all the seniors—had a ball watching it. We had so much fun and they busted my chops all night.
It was once-in-a-lifetime opportunity, and despite the loss, I
wouldn't have traded it for anything.

The Bus Leads to Retirement

One day in the middle of the winter, I was working as the AD and
I needed four buses for the next day's games. We had our own
bus, but I had two games and I couldn't rent another bus. It was-
n't that I couldn't get buses, but we were always third or fourth
in the pecking order, and the companies didn't have drivers.

I was sitting in my dining room, I was 63 years old, and I was
trying to get buses. I thought, what am I doing?

So I said to my wife Agnes, I'm going to retire.

She looked at me and asked, "When did you make this decision?"

I said, "Just now."

It wasn't a tough decision. You know, I had done the job, or any combination of jobs, for the past 18 years. I had done everything in the school, guidance counselor, coach, teacher, AD, coached three sports. I just hoped to get a good replacement.

Unfortunately, we had three consecutive losing seasons, from 2002 to 2004. We simply had one of those runs, which BC High had from time to time during my career, where we didn't have any dynamic skill players. We had good players, but nobody who was going to knock your socks off. In those years, we went 4-7 each year; we were never blown out, but we simply had one of those runs where we didn't have enough talent.

CHAPTER SIXTEEN

GUIDANCE COUNSELOR

Cotter was truly in his element when he became a guidance coun-cilor. In helping his student-clients get into the best schools possible, Cotter was able to use the connections he developed as a football coach. His strong relationship with the admissions officers of some of America's best colleges dovetailed with his coach's ability to see a kid's true potential. If a student was a client of Cotter's—and Coach did-n't just handle the athletes—Cotter would go the extra mile to help in any way he could.

Here's a personal example from Brendan Hughes: "Jim was my guidance counselor, and I wasn't sure where I wanted to go to school. I was up in the air between Holy Cross and Bowdoin. Bowdoin was a little bit of a reach for me, and although I played football for Jim, I was a special team's guy and a reserve defensive end, so I wasn't going to attract the attention of any college coaches. Eventually, I decided to apply early to Bowdoin, and in large part, because of Jim's hard work on the phone with the Bowdoin admissions department and with the BC High/Bowdoin alumni connection, I was accepted. Jim told my father it was the right school for me, and that's where I'd probably end up going. He felt it was the best fit for me, and he couldn't have been more on the mark. Jim's almost intuitive grasp of guidance has always impressed me a great deal."

Finding the School That Fit

When I went into guidance, I tried to make clear to the kids that I'll help you, the student, as much as I'll help the athlete, although I was well aware that it sometimes seemed, especially to non-athletes, that I did more for the athletes. That was true from only one standpoint: for an athlete there was simply more to do. I made sure that the athletes were looking at colleges where I thought they could play, but just as important, where I thought they would fit. I could make personal phone calls to the coaches. I made it a point to know who handled the BC High applications in every college I dealt with. I could talk to someone personally about XYZ and that was a big advantage in my ability to place kids. Just like back in my brief insurance career, I valued the personal touch much more than just simply writing letters. It worked. I was able to place a ton of kids into schools that they normally might not have been accepted into. I did write letters for kids, but in all honesty, I didn't really think they did all that much good.

I'll give you an example. I got a kid, one of my players, John Nerbonne, into Amherst. Rick Murphy, our quarterback, was accepted early decision to Amherst, which was where Nerbonne also wanted to go. I called one of their big alums and tried to sell him on Nerbonne. He told me that Amherst will never take two kids from the same Catholic high school. So, armed with that advice, I turned it around, and I called the admissions office and spoke to "John Glockester the third." That wasn't his real name, I don't even remember his name, but that was the name I used to refer to all those Ivy League type admissions guys. I told him that I had heard from an alumnus who told me Amherst would never take two kids from the same Catholic high school. He flatly denied it. "Oh, that's not so." Oh no, well from that point on, I was going to build a file, to the point where they can't refuse to take Nerbonne. Besides, he was a much better student than Murphy. Not as good an athlete, although he was a good football player, and good enough to play for them. So I kept contacting this guy. I used him as the advocate for Nerbonne. I'd call and say, hey John, Jim Cotter again from BC High, I just want to let you know that John Nerbonne got all A's in his mid-year exams. John Nerbonne got all A's and a 4.3 in the third quarter. They didn't accept him until the very last day that letters could go out. He got his letter April 14. He brought it to me, and I called the guy and said: "Geez, that alumnus was wrong. You guys took two kids from the same Catholic institution. Congratulations, and I'm glad you did, it restores my confidence in the private colleges."

I used the guy again and again. Some guys stay forever in those admissions jobs; other guys stay two years then go somewhere else. But in this case, it worked beautifully.

That also convinced me the personal touch was what got kids into school, not the letters that I wrote. One of the nicest compliments I ever received as a guidance counselor came from a kid who wasn't an athlete. I had many kids who weren't athletes, but, like I said, the perception was I was only really interested in helping the athletes. After I retired, I came back to fill a guidance position for a counselor who went on sabbatical. This one particular kid's case was a lot of work. He wanted to go to Harvard, and he was accepted. Afterwards, he came to me and said, "I want to apologize to you. When you took over my case, I said to myself, I'm screwed. He only helps the jocks. Not only did you help me, but you went the extra yard for me. So I want to apologize to you for thinking the worst about you."

A lot of college admissions officers, and coaches, were so good to us over the years. If you're talking about some of the things I did, then you've got to talk about some of the things other people did for us.

A couple of admissions people, and a couple of coaches, were really outstanding. Billy Fitzsimmons, of Harvard University, was one of those. When I moved to Weymouth, the local store was Joe's Corner Store, which was owned by Joe Fitzsimmons, who was Bill's father. I shopped at the store, of course, and Billy used to work for his father behind the counter. So I knew him since he was a little middle school kid. He later went to Archbishop

Williams High School, where he was a terrific goalie, and then went to Holy Cross and played hockey up there. After graduation, he was hired as an associate director of admissions at Harvard. When he was first there, I didn't deal directly with him, but I'd always call him for advice. I used to deal with Jack Reardon, who was the director of admissions, and when Jack was named athletic director, Bill took his spot and started handling the BC High applications. Over the years, I don't know what number of kids we got in through Billy, but he would handle all the BC High applications. Time and again, I would get Billy on the phone, we would talk about particular cases, and he really listened. He took some kids that Harvard might not have taken, except for my relationship with him. They all survived, all did well, and all have done well since they graduated.

Here's a funny story regarding Billy. One of our teachers, Tony Toto, who still teaches at BC High in the biology department, is a graduate of Harvard, class of 1970. Well, when his son Jeff was a senior at BC High, and was applying to Harvard, I said, "Tony, you know, you can't take any chances with Harvard admissions. Go over and see Bill. So I sent Jeff over to Fitzy, and Tony went with him. When they got to the interview, Bill told Tony that he could sit in on the interview.

So Tony sits in, and Billy asks Jeff about his SAT scores.

Jeff tells him, "Well, I have a 780 in verbal, an 800 in math, and I also have 800 in one of my science achievements."

And Billy says, "Why did Cotter send you to me? Normally, he sends me the kids with 550's!"

I just wanted to make sure Jeff got in. In fact, Jeff is now teaching English at BC High. Even though he was the dean of admissions for Harvard, Billy was a really fair guy, and I just wanted to make sure Jeff got in. He understood that when I was pushing a kid, there was more to him than just the numbers on a transcript. He was very generous with us, and I am very grateful.

Another guy, who no longer coaches but was one of my all-time favorite coaches, is a guy named Bill Macdermott, the former football coach at Wesleyan University. He was just a great guy. He never wore the fancy uniform. He always wore a pair of old Wesleyan sweatpants that would have the jock hanging out. He took every kid I ever recommended. He had a great rapport with the admissions office. Whenever we would recommend a kid, Bill would get him in, and many of these kids were not the type of kid Wesleyan normally would take. A lot of them were low 3.0, 3.1 GPA kids. I remember a late season visit to Wesleyan, which was like a BC High football reunion.

One year, one of my assistants, Bob Lynch, and I went down for a visit on a Friday afternoon. Catholic Memorial was playing Xavier High School of Middleton, Connecticut, in the evening, so we figured we'd go and scout the game. Before we went to the game, we went over to the season-ending practice of Wesleyan that afternoon. They had a big bonfire after practice, and it was a great finish to the season. Anyway, after practice, we grabbed the 10 BC High kids who were on the team and took them out for a quick bite to eat. Then all 12 of us went over and scouted CM. That was the year we ended up beating CM 7-6, and went on to win the 1977 Super Bowl Championship.

Powerful Words Still Ring True

On April 5, 2008, BC High had what we call the 3 and 8 reunion. The Classes of '63, '68, '73, '78, '83, and '88 were all there. It was based on a luau theme, so nobody had to get dressed up. There must have been 350 people there, and probably half of them I had as either students in history, counselees, or as students I'd coached in football, baseball, or basketball.

I had a crowd in front of me all night long. My daughter Grace was there with me and at the end of the night, around 10:30, the crowd was gone. I said to Grace, let's wait a couple of more minutes, and then we'll scram. Just then up walks a well dressed, small Italian kid, and he introduces himself. I don't want to use his name, but here is what he said.

"The only reason I'm here tonight is because of you. I waited all night until the line was gone because I wanted to talk to you alone. I don't drink, but I was standing over at the bar drinking coke, and I'm about to burst. I had you as my history teacher in 1961. You didn't know this, but I was from the worst section of East Boston, and I only came to BC High because my pastor gave me a scholarship.

"I wanted you to know, at that time in my life, I was shooting heroin, and the things you said to us in that history class: about what we could make of ourselves, that we were not worthless people, that we were bright enough to make a difference in the world, made a strong impression on me. Nobody had even spoken to me like that. You spoke to us in ways no one ever had before.

"It made such an impression on me that, during the summer between my sophomore and junior years, I got myself cleaned up. I graduated, went to college, have earned two Ph.D. degrees, and I now run a security company that operates using the latest techniques, featuring eye recognition. I also live in a community where my kids can grow up in a far different neighborhood than I grew up in East Boston, and they won't be challenged like I was and damaged as youngsters.

"I wanted to come here tonight and I wanted to tell you that story. I want to thank you for saving my life."

Isn't that amazing? I thought Grace was going to start bawling.

Waldo Kicks His Way into BC

Brian Waldron was a kicker for me, and a defensive back, at BC High, class of '79, and a real good athlete. He was also a catcher on the baseball team. After high school, he went up to prep school, and I was still doing his college placement work. Anyway, he called me one day in late January, or early February, and he said, "BC is starting to recruit a kicker." I told him that was inaccurate. He remained adamant that they were. So I called an assistant coach I dealt with, a nice guy, and he confirmed what Waldron had heard. He said they hadn't gotten their first choices, so they had reopened the recruitment process.

I asked who they were looking at. He told me the best one around seemed to be a kid from Dover-Sherborn High School. I knew the kid. I was one of the Shriners All-Star Game coaches that previous spring, and I had picked the kicker for the game for the south squad. The kid we picked was the same Dover-Sherborn kid BC was looking at. We chose him simply because he was the best of a bad lot of kickers. He couldn't touch Waldron. So I told the coach, "Look, Brian Waldron is so much better than that kid. Brian is at prep school this year, so he hasn't signed on with anybody." When I told him that, he told me to send some film. I told him that film on kickers isn't very reliable, why don't I just have him come out and kick for you? He told me he couldn't do that because it was illegal. I said, "The gate to the stadium is open, isn't it?" He said it was. So, I said, "Why don't I just bring him over there with a bag of balls, and you sit up in the stands and watch him kick."

Brian was off for February vacation. The coach agreed, and set it up for the following Monday. I told him we would be there.

At five o'clock that Monday morning, the day of the tryout, I get a phone call. It's Waldron.

"Coach, it's snowing out."

"Yeah?"

"Well, you know, how can we kick in the snow?"

"Look, Brian, we've got one shot. Either we do it today or we don't do it at all. So you get over there with your father and brother and shovel out spots every five yards, from the 10 to the 40 yard line, left hash, middle, right hash. We're kicking today."

Once everyone was there, and everything was shoveled off, I went and got the coach.

Brian loosened up, and when I felt that he was ready, I told him okay, "Let's go!" I held, and his brother and father shagged balls. We kicked left, center, right from the 10 to the 40. He didn't miss one. He also did a couple of kick offs and he almost kicked to the end zone. When it was over, they went off in their car, and I walked over to the coach. "Well, what do you think?"

He told me Brian was much better than the Dover-Sherborn kid, and that they would take him, and BC gave him a scholarship. He kicked all four years for BC, and he now works as a court officer in Marlborough.

CHAPTER SEVENTEEN

STANDOUT STUDENTS

Curtis Sturdevant was a kid who had been homeless in middle school. I knew that because one of my former history students taught him at a middle school in Boston. So, my former student called and told me he'd like to bring Curtis over. He told me Curtis wasn't a very good student. He said I'd have a hard time getting him in, but that he'd like me to try. So, he brought this kid over. Curtis was a little chubby, roly-poly, black kid and kind of shy, with his head down. He wouldn't look you in the eye. We talked. I really liked the kid. He said, "If you get me in here, I'd really appreciate it." He was a kind of mumbling type of kid. We got him in through the back door, with the promise that we would keep an eye on him. Freshman year, he barely got by. I was constantly going to his teachers.

We made sure we got Curtis with good teachers who cared about him. He got through freshman year and he also played football. Sophomore year, he played on the sophomore team, then junior and senior year, on the varsity. He was starting fullback as a senior, the blocking fullback. Curtis was not much more than your average high school football player, but the more you saw this kid, the more you liked him as a person, a student, and an athlete. He worked awfully hard to get to where he wanted to go.

Curtis came from nowhere—he literally was living in a car during middle school. There wasn't any father in the picture. His mother kept everything together. I don't know how they did it, but they somehow survived. It also didn't cost them any money to attend BC High. The school gave him a lot of financial help.

The guys, a lot of my former athletes, chipped in and paid for his tuition. So by the time senior year rolled around, his grades got better, and he had about a 2.8 average. I told him you are going to the University of Rochester.

I asked, "What do you think about that?"

He said, "What kind of school is it?"

I told him it's probably one of the best 25 schools in the country. It's a school a kid with your grades should never get into, but there's a chance to make it. Rochester's vice-president of enrollment services is Jim Scannell, one of my former football players. He'll take any kid I recommend.

I asked Curtis, "Are you going to go?"

He said, "Okay."

So he goes up there and all the BC High kids who are already up there, including my nephew, Mike Benson, look after Curtis. They get him in the right fraternity. And he ends up becoming president of the student body.

I remember during his junior-senior summer, Curtis came to see me, and he's driving a Sting-Ray.

I said, "You didn't steal any of the student government money, did you?"

"Oh no, my mother's got a good job now and she brought it for me."

What a success story. He was one of the most well liked kids on the campus. He is one of the all time great success stories at BC High. Last I heard, he was gainfully employed and living in New Hampshire.

Leo Smith Rescued from the Clutches of UCLA

Leo Smith was one of my best players. He was a 1977 All-Scholastic running back, and the Boston Globe's Massachusetts Player of the Year, who also led the state in scoring. Early in the summer, before Leo's All-Scholastic senior year, we set up a game plan to handle the recruiting process. It really came down to Leo's decision to stay local. We had narrowed it down to BC or Harvard. If he got a scholarship, he'd go to BC; if he could get into Harvard, he'd choose Harvard. Those were the two schools we really shot for, and he got into both.

But in the recruiting process, after his senior year, he made a visit to UCLA, and he saw Hollywood, the blond coeds, and all of a sudden the game plan changed. So he decided he was going to go to UCLA. He had to go out there in early August, because they were playing in the now defunct "Kickoff Classic" and practice started early. Once he was there, he realized that UCLA football wasn't for him.

At that time, I was visiting my wife Ann in the hospital, and I got a message to call Leo at noon our time. I remember he was staying on the tenth floor of a dormitory, and UCLA was watching him closely because they knew he wanted to leave, and they didn't want to lose him. The message said, "Coach, you've got to get me out of here. I want out."

So my friend, Jack Deneen, who worked at Polaroid as the finance director, had a friend who worked in the Polaroid office out in Los Angeles. He bought a ticket for Leo, and Leo flew out of there the next day. While all that was going on, I made calls to Harvard and BC. It turned out that BC still had one scholarship left and they gave it to Leo. Harvard also said they would accept him if he enrolled by September 1, but he chose BC because he didn't want his family to have to pay the $10,000 to go to Harvard.

Smith's version of why he chose UCLA differs slightly. He said that he went out there for a recruiting trip, and while he was there, he watched a USC/UCLA basketball game, a spring baseball game, and all the other niceties recruiters lay on their recruits. Smith returned home on a Sunday night and the following Monday, it began to snow, developing into a little local storm known as "The Blizzard of '78." After shoveling his driveway for the hundredth time over a four-day period, Smith decided he wanted to go someplace warm, and so he credits the blizzard with his initial decision to choose UCLA.

Recruiting Wars and the Notre Dame End Around

In 1979, Bob Clasby and Jack Shields were both seniors and were both being recruited by Notre Dame. Notre Dame loved Clasby from his junior films, and, early on, he made the commitment that he was going to sign with them. After some work, I also got them to sign Shields. Notre Dame had an offensive line coach by the name of Joe Yonto and he was a survivor, having survived four different coaches. He had been there about 20 years. He had two linebackers in his sights, Jackie Shields and some other kid somewhere. I knew, just by the tenor of his recruiting of Shields, that the other guy was his first choice. But he kept telling me, if Jackie Shields is accepted, I can get him a scholarship.

I said, "Joe, are you telling me, that if he's accepted, you'll scholarship him?"

"Absolutely," he said. "If he gets accepted, we'll scholarship him."

Now unbeknownst to me, after the football season, Jackie's father asks him to take a day off from school and go out to Notre Dame on a Tuesday and Wednesday. It is a time when there is no football being played, and it's not a recruiting weekend, so there are no stars in the eyes. His father wants to see if Jack is still comfortable out there when there is no football going on.

So, out Jackie goes. The admissions office arranges for him to stay with somebody and he has an interview with an admissions guy named T.J. Nokes.

When Jack comes back to school on a Thursday, he comes into my office and tells me he had gone out for a visit to Notre Dame. On Monday, Yonto is coming to BC High with scholarship papers for Clasby to sign. Now it's Thursday. We talk about the trip and he mentions that he interviewed with T.J. Nokes and that the two of them really hit it off. He tells me what a great guy he was, and that he was coming to Boston to run the marathon that year. He told Jack he'd love to talk to me about running the marathon.

So I asked, "You hit it off real well?"

He told me he did and that he was very positive about his application.

So he leaves and now my wheels are spinning. I call T.J. Nokes.

I say, "T.J. Nokes, Jim Cotter from BC High," and we talked about the marathon for about 20 minutes. Then I said, "I've got a bit of a problem with your coach Joe Yonto. To be honest with you, I think he's stringing me along about Shields. I know what he's doing; he's got two kids on the line, and he wants the other kid to go first and they're probably both in the same academic situation. He keeps telling me that if Jackie Shields is accepted that he'll scholarship him. I know Jackie said you two hit it off really well so I'm going to ask you a question. Is Jackie Shields accepted? If you tell me yes, I'm going to call Yonto because he's coming here next Monday with scholarship papers for Bob Clasby to sign, and I'm going to tell him to bring papers for Shields as well."

Now, I like this guy, and I've got the feeling he's a guy like me coming in to run the marathon. So I ask him the question, and he pauses, then he says, "Yes."

"Yes, what?"

"Yes, he's accepted."

"Is that 100 percent acceptance?" I ask.

"Absolutely, I'm the Eastern coordinator. By three o'clock this afternoon, that letter will be in the mail, so Shields will get it tomorrow or Saturday morning."

Then I ask him to transfer me to the football office. I ask for coach Yonto. They tell me that Coach Yonto isn't there. He's down in New Orleans on a recruiting trip and won't be back until the middle of the next week. Well, I ask for the number of the hotel where he is staying in New Orleans. They tell me they aren't sure if they have the liberty to give me that number.

Well, I explain the situation: about how Yonto is coming to Boston Monday to sign Bob Clasby, and I tell them I have just talked to the admissions office about the other boy I have, Jack Shields. Coach Yonto told me if Shields is accepted, he's going to get a scholarship, so I want to tell him to make sure he brings the papers for Shields as well. After listening, they give me the number.

I call and leave a message. Yonto calls me back.

"Jim, this is Joe. I'm coming Monday."

I tell him, "Good, Joe, now bring Shields' papers also."

There's a pause, "Well, I can't do that. I told you, we can't scholarship him until he's accepted."

"Oh, he's accepted," I say.

"Really? When did that happen?"

I tell him I'd spoken to T.J. Nokes that morning and he said an acceptance letter was in this afternoon's mail. "Jackie's accepted, and you always told me once he got accepted you'll scholarship him," I say. "So bring the papers for him also."

He didn't have a choice, and that's how Shields went to Notre Dame.

Chapter Eighteen

TRAGEDY AND REDEMPTION

Cotter's wife Ann suffered terribly from depression, which greatly attributed to her disease of alcoholism. Her children, Grace, Kelly, and Michael, often wonder how different their mother's life might have been been, if she had access to today's medical advances, and breakthroughs, for the treatment of depression. Unfortunately, that wasn't possible. Her disease had a draining effect on the entire Cotter family. Ann was given all the medical help one could offer, but she was never able to escape the clutches of her disease. Jim and his family struggled and, ultimately, persevered. Cotter did his best not to let the difficulties of his home life interfere with his duties as a father, teacher, or coach. He also found the sport of running and used it as a stress release that helped him cope with the situation at home. Ann's spirit and body eventually succumbed to the disease. Shortly after her death, Cotter met Agnes Donahue and the two have been happily married for 25 years.

Cotter said he never really had a definitive answer as to the reasons for Ann's drinking. Several circumstances might have played a contributing role. He thought that the move from Savin Hill to Weymouth, combined with what Cotter feels was his first wife's sense of low self-esteem, played a role in her addiction.

In the mid-seventies, Ann's drinking became serious, and her alcoholism affected our whole family in almost everything we did. Suddenly, we didn't go out much anymore, because everywhere we went, she'd be a problem. I had groups of Savin Hill friends I still saw, even though we were living in Weymouth. We had a vibrant social life, not that I had a lot of time, but when I had a night off, we'd go see friends. I was also pals with two different groups, the athletes and the non-athletes. In fact, Ann's best friend, Ann Clark, married this guy George Kenney, who was from my crowd. We used to see them socially at different house parties. But when we'd go to someone's house, I'd end up dragging Ann out. She'd be yelling, "I'm not going home with him, he's a jerk." It would be all of a sudden too; there was never any warning.

Ann hated moving to Weymouth. She felt that way from the day we moved. She was always mad about that. She wanted to go back to Savin Hill. I didn't. Looking back with the luxury of hindsight, maybe we should have stayed in Savin Hill, but at the time the future was very uncertain.

Ann's drinking was really difficult, and I'll give you an example. Grace was going to be the graduation speaker at Notre Dame High School in Hingham. Ann was probably as handy a woman as I've ever known. She could sew, make clothes, knit, do it all. Six months before the graduation, she started to make Grace's white graduation dress. Well, we were all so busy, I guess we just assumed it was made. On the morning of the graduation, Grace came down the stairs crying. Ann was just getting out of bed, struggling from another hangover. Well, Grace was crying because not only wasn't the dress finished, it was in six pieces.

Remember, this was the morning of graduation. I called Leo Smith's mother, Arlene, who lived up the street. In fact, I often sent the kids over there when Ann was in one of her drunken rages. Grace went over with the six dress pieces and Arlene put it together. It took her three hours and was a lot of work. Grace went and spoke at the graduation, and when we came back for the graduation party, Ann was not doing very well. This time, even her parents witnessed her behavior, and seeing her at that time was when she was at her very worst.

Over the course of her drinking years, Ann spent several stints in rehab hospitals. There were times when we were close to getting a divorce. But just before it got to that final point, she'd always say that she would do better, and I'd take her back and give her another chance. But it was a Catch-22. What do you treat first, the depression or the drinking? You can't successfully treat the depression if you continue to drink. We, as a family, did all that we could to help her. She spent many lengthy periods at McLean's Hospital, which is one of the clinical leaders in the treatment of people with depression. We had many family sessions regarding our family situation, and there was never any question that Ann was sick. We tried to help by providing Ann with the best professional treatment possible. She was a wonderful wife and mother, until she got sick. It was a shame that her alcoholism overwhelmed her and fractured our home life.

In 1983, on the Monday before Thanksgiving, Ann Cotter collapsed in her Weymouth home and died on the floor of her living room from massive internal bleeding as a result of her alcoholism. She was 44 years old.

The End of the Smokes and a Marathon Fix

I started jogging in the seventies. Initially, I started running to help with my mental health because of the problems at home. When I started running, I began with Jack Deneen and Arthur Bradley. They were training for the 1976 Boston Marathon and I'd run along with them. They'd humor me. They'd run me a couple of miles, and that was as far as I could go. Then they'd take off and do another 13 miles.

Now, I'm getting aggravated at myself, because I wanted to run more.

I decided if I wanted to run more, I'd have to give up cigarettes. On Ash Wednesday 1976, two months before the marathon, I quit smoking. I had tried to quit three previous times. I'd give them up for Lent, and each time I ended up going back on Easter Sunday. I'd go over to my uncle's house for Easter dinner, and he'd give me a cigar, and on the drive back home, I'd have three cigarettes.

This time it was for good, and two Sundays later, I joined Arthur and Jack who were going out to Hopkinton to run from the town center to Wellesley Center. They told me that I'd never make it. Arthur's wife Marylou was going to follow in her car and provide water stops, so I told them, if I can't make it, I'll get in the car with Marylou and we'll meet you there. Well, I made it. I had just run 12 or 13 miles and only nine days before I couldn't do more than a couple. That convinced me; I wouldn't smoke again.

My running became serious and I set the goal of running the Boston Marathon the next year. It turned out that the winter of 1977 was a very cold one for training. I don't think I ever broke a sweat during our 20-mile runs. On the day of the race, as it can often be in Boston, it was hot. I don't know if I didn't take enough water, because I never really had to in the winter, but at 16 miles, I started to cramp in my hamstrings. I shortened my stride almost to nothing, because when I reached my foot out, I'd feel the cramp, and it was an awful pain.

I ran with a kid named Eddie Costello from Savin Hill who was one of the all time funny little sons-of-a-gun. About a month before the race, I met him at Connors' and he said, "Jimmy, I hear you're going to run the marathon."

I said, "Yeah."

"Who are you running with?"

I told him I was running with a bunch of guys from BC High.

"How about I see you out at Hopkinton, and we'll run together?"

"Why not?"

I figured to myself, not a chance. When we get out there everybody is hopping in with the good runners. Not me, I'm going to the back of the line where I belong. Well, wouldn't you know, isn't Eddie there? We had more good times in that race than anybody. When we went by the girls of Wellesley—in those days, before they blocked them off with metal barriers, the girls would stand out in the middle of the road and the runners ran through this corridor of screaming, cheering women. So we ran through the line, and Eddie says, "Wasn't that great? Let's do it again." So we went back and did it again. A little while later, I started getting my cramps. That race was also the year that they filmed Paul Newman's wife Joanne Woodward in the movie, *See How She Runs*. It was something about a woman who gets divorced and decides that she is going to run the Boston Marathon.

Anyway, Eddie and I are approaching the beginning of Heartbreak Hill and my legs are really killing me, cramping and everything. He's kind of grabbing me by the arm, saying, "C'mon. C'mon you can do it! We can't drop out!"

Then, all of a sudden, behind us there's a huge cheer. And somebody on the sidewalk says, that's Joanne Woodward, she's coming. Now, we look up ahead and there are guys at the base of Heartbreak Hill with movie cameras. Eddie says to me, "There's no way two guys from Savin Hill are going to be seen walking in the marathon." He's dragging me along, and I'm laughing. And the movie guys are yelling, get out of the way. And Eddie's yelling, "Screw you! There's no way two guys from Savin Hill are going to be seen walking in the marathon."

Unfortunately, we didn't make it into the scene; we ended up on the cutting room floor. But I think it was the hills that probably helped me out, because my hamstring loosened, and once I got by BC, I was okay and finished in a very respectable time of four hours, twelve minutes.

I was in better shape the next year, but I stupidly did the carbohydrate loading diet. You know the one where you don't eat anything with carbs on day 6, 5, 4, then on day 3, 2, 1 you load up. Well, whether that had anything to do with it, I don't really know, but I came down with the flu on Friday and was sick as a dog. I was still sick Saturday, and on Sunday I felt a little better. But nevertheless, all I could eat was soup. On the day of the race, I still wasn't feeling that well. I went out to Hopkinton and ran, but when I got to the 16-mile mark, I began to get the chills. It was a cold and wet day and the guys I was running with had a water station located there with Arthur Bradley's wife Marylou. I thought if I don't get out now I'd never make the next 10 miles. So I dropped out, and Marylou drove me to the finish line, and I never attempted another Boston, but at least I have the one that I completed, and that one was certainly memorable.

A New Love and Relocation

Shortly after Ann's death, I met Agnes Donahue. Agnes, who is 11 years younger than I, grew up on Sudan Street in Dorchester, which was about a 25-minute walk to BC High. I knew Agnes. I had met her at various family gatherings. We met socially for the first time on the first day of Christmas vacation. Tommy Benson, now my brother-in-law, and I, were out Christmas shopping all day. When we finished, we went back to his house and had a few beers to relax. I was about to go home when Tommy's wife Mary, Agnes' sister, said, "Why don't you come over to Agnes'?" She lived across the street from them and was having a small party, so I agreed and tagged along. When the night was winding down, I asked Agnes if she had a boyfriend. It turned out she had just bro-ken up a relationship with a guy. I asked if she wanted to go out on a date and she accepted.

I was going on a trip to Memphis for the bowl game with BC, which turned out to be the "Ice Bowl." We had a crew of 13 piled into a Winnebago, and I had more laughs on that trip than I had had in years. When I got back, I again started dating Agnes and on New Year's Eve, after we had gone out for less than a week, I asked her if she wanted to get married. Six months later, on June 15, we were married. We've been married 25 years now, and it's been great. It was one of those things that I knew was right, from the beginning

Now we had to decide where we wanted to live. I was fortunate that my house in Weymouth was all paid for. I was always good at paying off the bills. Whenever I could, I'd put the extra hundred a month away toward the payment. Paul Hunter's wife, Joan, was a real estate agent, and she was able to sell my house. So now I had eighty-five grand in my hand, and I had to decide what I was going to do. I owned a house in Falmouth, and Agnes owned a two-family in North Quincy. I told her if I was going to live in the North Quincy house, we were going to need more room. We decided to add a big family room, off the kitchen, and we also remodeled the kitchen.

I wanted to give the kids something to remember their mother by, so I gave them the Cape house. Agnes and I bought another house in Falmouth, four tenths of a mile from where the kids are.

We lived in North Quincy for the first 10 years of our marriage, but then we decided we wanted to buy a single family house. We were looking around for another house and found this house in Wollaston during one of our boulevard walks, which we often took on Saturday mornings. On this Saturday, the weather played a role in our discovery. Normally, when we walk, we walk on the beach side, but on this particular day, it was as windy as a politician, and the sand was blowing in our faces. So we walked on the house side of the boulevard. As we were walking by this one area, we noticed a guy down the street putting a "For Sale" sign up in the yard. We went around the corner and when we got there, he was painting the back door. We inquired about the house, and he said there was an open house scheduled for Sunday. We asked if we could look at the house now. He said that wouldn't be fair, but come early Sunday morning. We were the first ones to see it, checkbook in hand. We loved it and gave him a deposit. I guess we were the high bidders.

We love the location, and since we've been here, we've made a lot of changes.

CHAPTER NINETEEN

RETIREMENT

When I retired as athletic director in 2000, I stayed on as football coach for four more seasons. I was 63 and I started taking my Social Security. I also had the Catholic Schools Retirement pension, which is lousy; it gives you only a week's pay. But I was still coaching, which helped supplement my income.

I also started running a week-long football summer camp in June 2002. It is a non-contact camp, five days, two-and-a-half hours on the field each day. I only send applications out to kids who have been accepted by BC High, particularly the seventh and eighth graders. I'll put the veteran coaches with the ninth graders. We take a total of 175 kids and give each kid two tee shirts and a nice pair of shorts. I pay the coaches a good salary for 20 hours of work. It works out well; the kids get their money's worth, and everybody's happy. We teach position technique. We teach all the positions, and I keep the groups small, a maximum of 15 kids per coach. The main reason I started the camp came from a parents' night. When I was the head coach for all those years, the mothers would come to me at parents' nights and say, "My Johnny never made the freshman team because he never played football, and he was competing against kids who played Pop Warner."

We go over all the techniques for any position the kid wants to play, so he's got an understanding and a better shot to play and make the team. And I think it works. You should see the improvement. They don't wear any pads and we're not banging heads, but I think it works out great.

Pride of the Eagles: Cotter Battles ALS

Cotter was diagnosed with ALS in October 2006. He has battled the disease the same way he has handled every facet of his life—good or bad—in a matter-of-fact manner. His friends refer to it as the "Cotter Way." He has carried on with his life in as normal a manner as possible, lunching with legions of friends, while continuing to raise money and represent the school he truly loves, BC High.

Up until the spring of '06, my legs didn't seem to be getting any worse. They were weaker, of course; I couldn't jog anymore, but I was still walking every day. But then, all of a sudden, in the late spring, early summer of 2006 I had to start using a cane. It was a combination of the legs getting weaker, as well as my balance simply being off; I felt unstable. Ironically, it wasn't until I started using the cane and had three falls at the Quincy Y in an eight-week period, that I realized something was wrong. All three times, I split my left elbow because I had the cane in my right hand, and each time I landed on my left hip. After every occurrence, I went to the Quincy City Hospital for stitches.

After the third fall, I decided to go to Mass General for an evaluation to figure out what was going on. The first guy I saw was a spine guy, Dr. Frank X. Pedlow. Over the course of two months or so, I saw him three times. I was introduced to him by Larry and Sean Foley, two of my former players, who sold medical equipment. I had two sets of x-rays looking for different things, and he told me there was nothing on the spine.

He recommended I go to see a neurologist. So I saw Dr. Stephen Parker from MGH in September 2006, and he did two different tests. One test was an EMG, a test used to determine if a patient has ALS. Dr. Parker said that in his opinion, I didn't have ALS, but he wanted me to see their ALS guy. I was thinking that it was either ALS or MS, one of those things that causes nerve damage. When he mentioned the word, it sounded a little more realistic.

I saw Dr. William David, who had just come to Boston from Minneapolis about two months earlier. He accessed the EMG test, and during our first meeting he was talking and talking and talking, and I finally said, "Hey, do I have ALS, or do I not have ALS?" I told him, just tell me, because he was just kind of beating around the subject. He told me, yeah, I had ALS.

So it wasn't a shock. I was obviously disappointed when they diagnosed it. But I guess I kind of surmised that was what it was going to be anyway. And then we went home. When we got home, Agnes started bawling because it's a death sentence. It might not be imminent, but it's rapidly progressive. The first thing Dr. David said to me was you won't experience any pain from ALS. That's not bad. When I told the kids, I just called them up and told them. Nobody, at least openly to me, broke down and started crying. I'm sure they all had a cry on their own time, but that was it. I said, "Okay, let's go on from here."

It would be easier to handle if you had some idea of how it was going to break down. Dr. David doesn't have the slightest idea what's going to happen to me tomorrow. Rick Kennedy, my physical therapist, who had a father and brother die of ALS, knows more about it than the doctor does. There really is very little the doctor can do for you. He prescribed one medication that has been approved by the FDA called Rilutek. It's supposed to slow down the degeneration of the nerves. Whether it does or not, I don't know. That's the only approved medication they have for ALS. They have a lot of research going on, but nothing has been proven.

ALS starts with your nerves, and the nerves die and your muscles follow, and they become debilitated. So, it's not fun to look forward to, but that could be years. We were out talking to Judge Bobby Kelly, who was two years behind me at BC High, and his first wife died in seven months from ALS. Nobody can tell you how it's going to happen. The voice, that's going to be the hardest, losing my voice.

I'm convinced that my illness started from the fertilizer we used on the football fields. Every year that I coached, when we started double sessions to get ready for the season, the maintenance crew was putting the final coat of fertilizer on the field. Remember Danny Allen, the Holy Cross coach? Danny died of a disease that crippled him, and he was convinced that fertilizer on the fields had something to do with it.

So far I've gone from a cane to a walker, which was the result of my third fall. The doctor from the emergency room at Quincy City Hospital was looking at my records. She said, this is the third time you've been here, and all three times, you've fallen using the cane, I suggest you get on the walker. Then, she said, this is going to happen more often, and you don't want to be stitching up that same elbow six or seven times. She also told me that I've got to stop falling because I could break my hip. Dr. David said the same thing to me the other day. He said, "Whatever you do, Jim, don't start screwing around without the walker. If you break your hip with ALS, you don't heal as well."

The walker wasn't demeaning, it was just, you know, once you're on it, you're going to be on it forever. So I fought it as long as I could, until I finally reached a point where I had no choice. Right now I couldn't walk across this room to that chair about six feet away without falling down. It's gotten that bad in just six months.

Treatment to Slow the Progress of ALS

The only treatment I receive is from Ratt "Rick" Kennedy of the Kennedy Brothers Physical Therapy. I see him twice a week and he works primarily with my legs and anything from the waist down. It's basically pushing, pulling, and stretching. We work on crossing my legs over, work on the hip, the foot, the toes, hamstrings, all the muscle groups. The more flexible you are, the less likely you are to freeze up, because if that happens, you won't be able to use your limbs. Once you lose something with this disease, you can't get it back. I work on muscle strength and flexibility. When Ratt is through, his assistant does a series of pushing exercises, and I work against him, pushing sideways, forward, and back, using various ball drills focusing on the core. That's what we do, and we do it twice a week.

I don't know if I'm any better than when I first went to him in April 2007, but it seems to help at least with my flexibility.

But I've declined since December 2007. I can barely get out of a chair even with the arm rests. I can barely push myself up, because it's all with my arms; the legs have no strength. It's more balance, my flexibility and balance, are just not good at all. In the last week, my walking has gotten worse, slower. Agnes and I, we're walking up to the Y gym, and I told her to go ahead because it was cold out that day. I told her I'd see her inside. All of a sudden, she's inside and I'm about one third of the way behind her. I'm just slower and it's noticeable. But that's what happens at some point, no question. I'll be in a wheelchair. Anyway, at the Y, I ride a recumbent bike for 30 minutes and I work about 40 minutes on the weights downstairs using a lot of dumbbells. I do curls, flys, triceps, as I work all the muscle groups in the upper body.

When I have to use a wheelchair, I don't think it will bother me at all. I will certainly get out. I will not become housebound. As I already said, I've never felt sorry for myself. I'm certainly not going to brood about my situation.

During the summer of 2008, Jim Cotter, his legs now so weakened that they could no longer support him, was permanently confined to a wheelchair. He has also lost the use of his arms and his hands while his voice has grown noticeably weaker.

I get calls from all over and I'm very happy to hear from people. It can be former players, former students. Everyone goes through something like this. A friend gets sick and you don't know what to do. Should I call him? Go over the house? See him once a week? So I know it's awkward for people when they hear, "Cotter's got ALS. What do I do?"

I got over 1,000 cards. I've got cards up the ying yang. I feel like putting out an e-mail, don't waste any more money on cards, give me a call for five or ten cents. I get a lot of calls. Most of them are, "We'd like to see ya, go out to lunch." I usually wait for them to call me back. I'm out to lunch almost every day. It's become our primary meal. It's really been a lot of fun.

I think it was during the last week of March when I got a call from Jerry York. He said he was coming over with a friend and they were going to take me out to Dunkin' Donuts for a coffee. I said sure. I coached Jerry in baseball at BC High, and at that stage of his athletic career, I think he was a better baseball player than a hockey player.

He shows up in this big black SUV. I said, "Jerry, I'll never be able to get into that, it's too high off the sidewalk."

"Don't worry Jim," he said. "We'll get you in."

Well, Jerry grabs one leg, and his pal grabs the other, and they try and lift me in. No luck. Then they try and back me in. Again, no luck. Finally, they decide they're going to push me from the back and drag me in that way. I still couldn't get in.

Finally, I say, "Look, there's a Dunky's just around the corner. Go grab some coffees and bring them back, and we'll have them in the house."

That's what they did, and we sat around and talked for about two hours.

Well, this past Tuesday [April, 8, 2008] the phone rings, and it's Jerry. He said, "How you doing, Jim."

"I'm fine, but where are you?"

"Oh, I'm about to get on the bus to take us to the airport for our trip to Denver." BC won that 2008 College NCAA Hockey Championship in Denver.

I said to myself, no way he's getting onto the bus. He's probably sitting in the office, and just saying he's about to get on the bus to keep the conversation short.

Well, that Friday, April 9, my daughter Grace ran her annual gala, which is a fundraiser for the Jesuits of New England. One of the attendees was Jack Dunn, director of the Office of Public Affairs for Boston College.

He comes up to me and says, "Hey, Jim, how do you know Jerry York?"

I said, "I used to coach him in baseball at BC High. Why?"

"Well, I was with him the other day, and just as he was about to board the bus, he said, 'I've got to make one more phone call,' and it was to you! I just wanted to know where the connection came from."

Things like that really mean a lot to me. It gives me a boost to know guys from BC High are always there for each other, that we never forget where we came from, and we never forget a friend.

The Surprise of Unexpected Help

Dr. Marty Dunn was two years ahead of me at BC High and is now a facial oral surgeon who also started Por Christo in South America. That was his gig. In fact, he even adopted one of the girls he worked on in the program.

Well, Marty and I worked together my junior year at BC High on a 30-day appointment from Dom Bianculli, on the State Highway Department. We went down to the Stoughton sand pit and the foreman was a friend of my uncle "Buddy" Hickey, and he kept me in the pit. He kept four of us: George Ramacordi, who became a coach of Milton High's football team; Jack Garrity, an All-America hockey player at Boston University and a member of the 1948 U.S. Olympic team who would later become the football coach at Quincy High; and Marty Dunn. We all stayed in the pit, and Ramacordi and Garrity drew football plays in the sand. I was the timekeeper, and Marty and I became friendly simply because we worked together for those six weeks.

Anyway, this past December [2006], Marty saw Grace at an affair and told her he had just had a barn on his property converted into a study and a library. He had two wonderful carpenters, young guys, and he'd like to use them to build a ramp for me on my house. Grace told him not to ask me, because I'd say no. He said to Grace, "I'm asking you." Grace told him yes, I'd love one. Grace knew I'd be too stubborn to accept his offer. So he sent the two guys to build it and they did. They built the ramp at his expense. These were the same two guys Agnes and I hired later to put in a walk-in shower we recently installed.

Marty's gift and kindness were a shocker to me. He is a very generous guy, and I can't thank him enough. In fact, I just sent out letters for our Hall of Fame dinner this November 2007. I'm giving Marty, not just for his generosity to me, but for his generosity to the school, one of the two "Man for Others Awards."

Marty's gift came out of the blue. At the time, I didn't think I needed it, but jeez, it wasn't even finished and I wasn't able to get up the stairs, so obviously I needed it.

Another surprise came from a former player, Frank Foley, who played for me in 1972. I was his counselor, too, and he was a wonderful kid. I loved him. He wasn't a great player but tumbled into a job and kept it through his senior year. He called me and said his father-in-law had passed away about six months earlier and he had a couple of things he thought I might need. He told me he had a scooter, an old lady scooter, but it will get me down to the beach when I'm at my place in Falmouth. He also had a stair chair. I priced everything: the scooter goes for about four grand and the chair for about five grand. This guy took the chair out of Frank's house and came here and installed it in 45 minutes.

The gifts were like manna from heaven. A lot of guys have money, but they don't give it to anybody. Other guys like Marty Dunn and Frank Foley will give you the shirt off their back.

Another gift came from Bob Howe, BC High '64, who is the president of Atlantic Data Services. In February of '07, Bob graciously provided his private jet and flew Agnes, Grace, and me to Naples, Florida, for a much needed winter mini-vacation.

Never Forget Your Roots

I'd always tell my players, don't forget where you come from. I used to say that to all my teams, don't forget where you come from. Don't forget BC High. You might strike it rich, but don't forget when you were here and didn't have anything. Guys like Jack McNeice and Jack Shaughnessy, they can't give enough money. Look at Marty Dunn. I worked with him for 30 days 53 years ago and in all those years, we've been involved with the BC High alumni. I don't think we said much more than, "Hi, Jim," "Hi, Marty," maybe small talk at a cocktail party. Guys like that, there're not many like them.

I'm happy to report that my scholarship fund is up to a half million dollars, and at that level it can sustain itself. My daughter Grace and Matt Curran from BC High sent out 90 letters to my former players with the goal of getting the Cotter scholarship up to $500,000, and the guys certainly came through. I'm very grateful to all who have contributed, and now we can help six or seven kids with tuition each year, and my money only goes to city kids.

I really believe in helping people. If my legacy is one thing, it is all the kids I helped at BC High, as a counselor and a coach. I tried to help people. I tried to give them the opportunity to become a little better than maybe they thought they could be.

It is impossible to summarize the effect a singular man from Savin Hill had on the lives of thousands of players, students, and friends. If you pardon the cliché, they broke the mold after they made Jim Cotter. He is a man who never sought the headlines; yet, he couldn't do enough for others. We won't see his likes again.

His spirit and persona is best captured in a scene painted by Pete Hamill in his tribute book, "Why Sinatra Matters."

Hamill recalls a late New York night, and sitting at a table, along with Sinatra, were legendary sports writer Jimmy Cannon, Sinatra's good buddy and confidant Jilly Rizzo, saloon keeper Danny Lavezzo, and William B. Williams, the disc jockey who christened Sinatra "The Chairman of the Board."

The table was filled with empty glasses, and stubbed cigarettes overflowed the ashtrays. The discussion turned to the merits of Hemingway versus Fitzgerald. Finally, Cannon asked Hamill what he thought. Hamill quoted something he was once told by Dizzy Gillespie: "The true professional can do it twice." Sinatra loved that and said, "Wow, is that true. That can apply to everything in life. That's a great line."

Well, just like the Chairman of the Board, Jim Cotter did "it" countless times, in many different venues, in many different ways, for many different people, and never for himself. He scraped and clawed his way from the working class streets of Savin Hill and the longshoreman docks of his father, into the classroom and onto the football field of BC High. Then he did the same at Boston College.

As a history teacher, coach, father, mentor, counselor, and friend, with a keen eye trained to look for the less fortunate, he guided literally thousands of kids onto the right path, toward a better life's journey. The father to three loving children and devoted husband to his wife Agnes, Jim Cotter has been able to make the world a better place for those who knew him. His lifelong friend and fellow coach, Frank Casey, expressed it perfectly, "Anybody can x and o, but he was the best I ever saw at getting kids into a great college." Yes, the Chairman would, indeed, tip his hat to Jim Cotter.

AFTERWORD

This book would not have been possible without the support of a cast that might be bigger than the one from the movie *Ben-Hur*.

First, my deepest thanks to Jim and Agnes Cotter for their kindness in allowing me to invade their privacy for nine months, and for their remarkable display of spirit, enthusiasm, and humor, often under very trying circumstances.

To Grace Cotter Regan or, as anyone who has known her since the days she slipped into the old BC High Eagle suit on the sidelines of her father's games, "Gracie," thanks for your editorial assistance and your steady guidance in keeping everyone on the right track. DT couldn't have done it any better.

To my No. 1 sounding board and good friend Bob McDevitt, who for 30 years has listened to more stories than a jailhouse guard but always provides concrete and well-thought-out advice.

To editor Brendan Hughes, who had his Columbia journalism-school degree severely tested, but magnificently piloted a raw manuscript away from the shoals and into clear sailing. "Brenny," like it or not, you have a pal for life.

To Joe Corcoran for his kind and very generous hand in shepherding this project into fast forward, thank you.

To editors Julie Michaels Spence and Vicki Sanders, a pair of real pros, for understanding and protecting the voice of Jim Cotter, while at the same time using a diamond cutter's skill to shape this book into a polished gem. To Tom Mulvoy, many thanks, Tom, for your advice and direction on the best way to attack this project.

During the two years Jim and I worked on this book, I spoke with almost all of his closest friends—a long list to be sure. Their generous, thoughtful input was an essential addition to the book. To Jim's lifelong pals, Tom Benson, Jack Deneen, Frank Casey, Bill O'Shea, Joe Sheehan, Bob Dunn, John Molloy, and Steve Hughes, thank you, guys, for offering advice and insight about your friend, while at the same time, doing what friends do, protecting his backside. Thank you, everyone, for your support regarding this project.

To Peter Williams for your support and wise counsel and to another pro, the Boston Globe's Mark Blaudschun, who helped me cut through the clutter.

To my pals Bill Griffin, Mike "Tucker" DeLuca and the Eire's John Stenson, thank you for your kind words of support. It meant a lot, and unlike a politician, I mean it.

To my mom, Terry Kenney, and her traveling partner Catherine Macheras, thanks for the unstinting support.

Heartfelt thanks to my best pal and my rock, my wife Carol, and my daughter Alex, who although they may roll their eyes at some of my ideas, are always there to listen and provide encouragement.

Thanks to Chris Lovett, the former editor of the Dorchester Argus Citizen, who was "foolish" enough to allow me to first put words into print, and to the Jesuits and teachers of BC High for providing me with an appreciation for the spoken, and written, word.

Finally, to the neighborhood of Dorchester, specifically the rectangle that runs from the Dublin House on Columbia Road to "old" St. Margaret's Parish to long gone Connors Tavern and down to the park at Savin Hill. From the early fifties to the mid-seventies, that area provided a Runyon-esque cadre of colorful characters, including one named Jim Cotter. This book would not have been possible without all of you.

—Paul Kenney

INDEX

SPONSORS

In gratitude for the generosity of Coach Cotter's friends, family, former players, coaches, colleagues, classmates, and teammates from Savin Hill, BCHIGH and Boston College who contributed to the project. Your gifts of time, talent, treasure, and friendship cannot be measured. Special thanks to the A Team who helped us make the Cotter Book Project a reality; Joe Corcoran, Jack Deneen, Ed Farley and Paul Kenney. And to our Unsung Heroes and Heroines whose gifts and support of the Cotter Book Project and the BCHIGH Cotter Scholarship have gone above and beyond the call of duty: Joe and Rose Corcoran, Dr. Gerry McGillicuddy, MD, John McNeice, John and Kathleen Murphy, Fred and Kathleen Knapp and Family and Jack McDonough! You are all "true men and women for and with others" and Coach's legacy will carry on because of your love and care.

AMDG

Grace Cotter Regan

Tony and Marilyn Abraham
William and Barbara Ahern
Tim and Erin Alberts
Joe and Lou Amendolia
Nick Argento, Jr.
Jack and Deborah Baronas
Jon and Julie Bartlett
William and Patricia Beck
Robert and Catherine Beniers
Bob Bennett
Karen and David Benson
Tom and Mary Benson
Tom and Fiona Benson
Mike and Ann Benson

Jay and Tracey Bernasconi
Myles and Virginia Berry
Kevin and Mary Berry
Dean Boylan, Jr.
Arthur and Marylou Bradley
Garrett and Heather Bradley
David J. Breen
Jack "Ace" Brennan
Mike and Julie Brennan
Bill Brennick, Esq.
Colleen Broderick
Dr. Mark and Patty Bulman
Tim Bulman
Bill and Ann Burke

Edward Cahill
Carol Cahill
Peggy Cahill
Sr. Nancy Cahill, SND
Ronan Campbell
Lawrence and Sarah Carlson
Mary "Sissy" Carr
Frank, Peggy, John Casey and family
Jim Cashin
Al and Ann Charron
Joseph Chase
Leonard, Kathleen, Sean and Christian Ciavarro
Dick and MaryJo Clasby
Joe and Joan Clifford
Jack Coleman
Mike Collins
Michael Connolly
Mark Conroy
Sindiah Conroy
Joe and Rose Corcoran
Joe and Gayle Corcoran
Leo and Sara Corcoran
Richard W. Corner, II
Paul Costello
Bill and Eileen Cotter and family
Dan and Samantha Cotter
Don and Peg Cotter and family
Frank Cotter
John and Mary Cotter and family
June and Peter Cotter-Lanctot
Kevin and Betty Cotter and family
Mike, Beth, Casey and Mikayla Cotter
Ted and Nancy Cotter and family
Ed Cronan
Bette Crowley
Bill and Laura Crowley

Jamie and Alex Crowley
Maggie Crowley
Tom Cunningham
Jim and Jean Curley
Lawrence R Curran, Jr.
Gerald Curtin
Paul and Janet Curtis
Albert J. DeLuca
John and Karen Deneen
Joe Devlin
Dennis and Peggy Dohery
Jedlie and Chris Doherty
Paul Dolan
Chris and Tia Doyle
J. Barry and Kathy Driscoll
Bob and Mary Dunn
Dr. and Mrs Martin J. Dunn
Kevin and Jean Dunn
Leo and Helen Dunn
Steve and Laura Durant
Joe Durant
Brian Durant
Michael Durant
William Dwyer
Larry and Lynn Eisenhauer
Michael Elliott
Paul Evangelista
Edward Farley
Kirk and Christine Farrell-O'Reilly
Michael Ferullo
Norm Fitzgerald
Tim Flaherty
Paul Flaherty
Carol Flaherty
Richard Flynn
Jeff Fleming
Frank and Jackie Foley
Larry Foley
Sheila and Larry Foley

Sean Foley

William C. Foley

Michael and Marian Foley

Steve Fratalia

Tim and Mary Freeman

Steve Fulchino

Rob and Ellen Crowley Fullerton

Jack Furey

Jim, Joanne and Nick Gallagher

Ron and Linda Gaudet

Luis and Suzanne Gonzales

Cesar & Gilda Gonzales

Mark Gorham

Mary Frances Greene

Robert and Susan Halkyard

Ken and Ann Halloran

Christoper Hamilton, Esq.

John Hanlon

Larry Hanson

Mary, Cathy, Joanne, Maureen
and Janice Hayes

Jim and Judy Hickey

Ron Hoffman, CCALS

Dick and Joan Horan

Robert and Janice Howe

Shaun Hubbard

Brendan Hughes

Steve and Clare Hughes

Pete Hughes

PJ and Beth Hussey

Mike Hussey

Kathy Hussey-O'Brien

Dan Johnson

Thomas J. Joyce

John Kelly

Bryan Kelly

Breton Kelly

Barry Kelly

Justin Kelly

Conor Kelly

Carolyn and Walter Kelly

Bill and Maureen Kemeza

John and Mary Kennedy

Ratt Kennedy

Paul and Carol Kenney

Mark Kenney

Dan Kenslea

Frank Keohane

Stephen Kiely

Paul and Claire Kingston

Tim, Kelly, Annie and Matt
Kostenbauer

Fred and Kathleen Knapp

John and Elizabeth Knapp

Eric and Heather Knapp

Dan Knapp

Linda Koenig

Kenneth J. and Virginia Langley

Kenneth Langley

David and Ann Langley

John Leahy

Jack Leonard

Anne Lewis

John and Laurie Lynch

Robert Lynch

Doug MacMillan

Don MacMillan, SJ

Bill and Gerry Madden

Noreen Maddox

Jack and Linda Maguire

Thomas J. Mahoney

Jim Martorano and family

Mass HS Coaches Association

Dave and Marjorie McDonogh

Jack McDonough

Gerald and Mary McGillicuddy

Michael and Kay McGonagle

Joseph McKenney

John and Joan McLoughlin

John McNeice

Paul and Michelle Meaney

Doc and Barbara O'Brien Miller

John and Betty Molloy and family

Jack and Kathy Molloy

Michael Moran

Gerard and Marianne Morelli

Jack and Mary Morris

Tom Mulvoy

Bo and Pat Mullane

Rick Murphy

John and Kathleen Murphy

Joyce, Wayne, and Matthew Murphy

Eileen Murphy

Bobby Muse

Michael Nerbonne

Matthew Nestor

John and Ann Marie Normant

John Norton

Tom Norton

Bob and Yolanda O'Brien

Dan and Karen O'Brien

Paul O'Brien

Jim O'Brien

Jim and Mary O'Connor

Thomas and Elizabeth O'Donnell

Bill and Gerry O'Shea

Reid Oslin

Jim and Christine O'Sullivan

Joseph Pedulla

Joe Petrowski

David and Jeanne Pratt

Ellen Pumphret

Carmen and Carol Quintiliani

T. David Raftery

Steve and Kathrine Ranere

Mark Reed

Grace, Bernie, Luke, and Moe Regan

James Regan

Arch and Kay Regan

Jim and Maureen Reynolds

Gene Roman and family

Charlie Rourke

James Rourke Rourke

Mark Rourke

Mary Rourke

Ned Rourke

Michael Sabina

Gil and Margaret Lynch Sakakeeny

Jim, Nancy, Jessica, and Jocelyn Scannell

Jack Shaughnessy

Dan Shea

John Shea

Joseph Sheehan

Jack Shields

Bill Shields

Tom and Mary Shields

John and Carmel Shields-Mannix

Jonathan Sloane

Kevin Smith

Leo Smith

Greg Smith

John and Elaine Smoot

Bill Stack

Tom Stack

Jane Staunton

Liam Staunton

Myles Staunton

John Stenson

Charlie Stevenson

Daniel and Lorraine Sullivan

Dan and Christine Sullivan
Dan Sullivan
Freddie Sullivan
Norm and Barbara Swain
Margie Tangney
Bernie and Barbara Taracevicz
Bernie, Jr. Taracevicz
Steven Taracevicz
Chris Taylor and Family
Joseph and Christine Tierney
Greg Timility
Joe and Elaine Timilty
Joe Timility
Bill and Mary Timmins
Jack and Janice Travers
Brian Waldron
Gregory and Tara Waldron
Xaverian Brothers High School
Jerry and Bobby York
Jack and Leez Yunits
David Zenga
Elaine Zingarelli

Gifts Made In Memory

Brody Varna Bartlett
Babsy Cahill
Bobby Conroy
Ann Cotter
Dixie and Les Cotter
Edward Cotter
Kyle and Sean Cotter
"The Commander" Bill Crowley
Colie and Mame Donahue
Suzanne Donlin Kelly
May and Tom Grace
Joseph P. McKenney
Chris Murphy
Kenny Murphy
Steve Trapilo
Catherine Shea
Uncle Shuggy Hugh Thompson

Testimonials

"A wonderful book about a Boston legend. As colorful, insightful, and enthralling as its subject. You'll end up buying two copies, one to read, one to pass on in hopes of inspiration."

—*Dennis Lehane, author of* Mystic River *and* Gone, Baby, Gone

"If they made a movie of *The Coach Jim Cotter Story*, the angels would have to return John Ford from eternity to direct this picaresque memoir of the life and times of a legendary Boston high school football coach. Ford—Francis Feeney, an Irish kid from Portland, Maine—would know just how to film it. He'd begin with the kid from Savin Hill 'over the bridge' who works with his father down on the Boston docks, who in summers plays football all day on the playgrounds and beach and up to his knees in the brine, who gets beat up by a gang from another neighborhood while in the men's room of the Upham's Corner theater while his girlfriend cools her heels in the audience waiting for her popcorn, an affront soon avenged in the exciting 'battle of the bridge.'

Ford would cast a Leo Gorcey-type as the young scrapper who parlays his athletic skills and his gritty character into a scholarship to Boston College High School, a Jesuit-run academic powerhouse, to which, after lettering in two sports at Boston College, he returns and stays as teacher, guidance counselor, athletic director, and beloved coach for over forty years. To play Coach Cotter, Ford would insist on Jimmy Stewart, who'd have one of the richest parts of his career—the life of a decent, dedicated, caring man who made a difference in hundreds of lives, teaching boys by his example how to be good men. And at the end of the picture, when the old coach is battling Lou Gehrig's disease with jaunty fortitude (having shown his players how to live, he shows them how to die) the now middle-aged players pitch in to fund a scholarship at BC High named after Jim Cotter that will keep alive his name and vocation—shaping destinies—for generations. The last scene, where the players announce their bequest in honor of the wheelchair-bound coach—well, when, after listening to the testimonies of what he meant to so many, Jim Cotter tries to acknowledge their tribute and gets choked up with emotion—there won't be a dry eye in the house."

—*Jack Beatty,* Atlantic Monthly *senior editor, NPR* On Point *commentator, and author of* Rascal King: The Life and Times of James Michael Curley

"If you are a fan of BC High football, this is a must read."

—*Mark Blaudschun,* Boston Globe *sports reporter*

"Every BC High student past, present, and future should read this book."

—*Charlie DePascale BC High '49*

"A must read for those who came under his guidance, and a textbook for those who are planning to teach, coach, or mentor."

—*Rocky Carzo, Tufts University athletic director emeritus*

"It reads like *Mystic River* without the crime, and it flows like butter."

—*Editor Julie Michaels Spence*

"A colorful read about an 'old school,' larger-than-life coach. Coach Cotter and guys like him taught us more about life, and what it takes to be successful in life, namely, work ethic, self discipline, and overcoming adversity, than anything we learned in the sterile environment of biology class. Those of us who were fortunate enough to play for guys like Jim Cotter are better off thanks to their influence and guidance."

—*Tim Murphy, Harvard University head football coach*